THE RACE TO RELEVANCE

THE RACE TO RELEVANCE

A NEW PARADIGM FOR BUSINESS AND PERSONAL SUCCESS

COLT BRINER

No part of this publication may be reproduced or distributed in any form or by any means, without the prior permission of the publisher. Requests for permission should be directed to permissions@indiebooksintl.com, or mailed to Permissions, Indie Books International, 2511 Woodlands Way, Oceanside, CA 92054.

The views and opinions in this book are those of the author at the time of writing this book, and do not reflect the opinions of Indie Books International or its editors.

Neither the publisher nor the author is engaged in rendering legal or other professional services through this book. If expert assistance is required, the services of appropriate professionals should be sought. The publisher and the author shall have neither liability nor responsibility to any person or entity with respect to any loss or damage caused directly or indirectly by the information in this publication.

S&P 500® is a registered trademark of Standard & Poor's Financial Services, LLC o
Indeed® is a registered trademark of Indeed, Inc.
Glassdoor® is a registered trademark of Glassdoor, Inc.
Nike® is a registered trademark of Nike, Inc
Dove® is a registered trademark of Conopco, INC.
Always® and P&G® are registered trademarks of The Procter & Gamble Company
LinkedIn® is a registered trademark of LinkedIn Corporation
Blockbuster® is a registered trademark of Blockbuster L.L.C.
Netflix® is a registered trademark of Netflix, Inc.
Toro® is a registered trademark of The Toro Company
Google®, YouTube®, and Nest® are registered trademarks of Google, LLC
Ring® and Whole Foods® are registered trademarks of Amazon Technologies, Inc
FaceTime® is a registered trademark of Apple, Inc.
Red Bull® is a registered trademark of Red Bull GmbH
Polaroid® is a registered trademark of Polaroid Corporation
Rolex® is a registered trademark of The Hans Wilsdorf Foundation
Casio® is a registered trademark of Casio Computer Co., Ltd
Shopify® is a registered trademark of Shopify, Inc.
Harley-Davidson® is a registered trademark of Harley-Davidson, Inc
Microsoft® is a registered trademark of Microsoft Corporation
Disney® is a registered trademark of The Walt Disney Company
Facebook® is a registered trademark of Facebook, Inc
Tesla® is a registered trademark of Telsa, Inc.
Coca-Cola® is a registered trademark of The Coca-Cola Company
Patagonia® is a registered trademark of Patagonia, Inc.
Allstate® is a registered trademark of the Allstate Insurance Company
Dick's Sporting Goods® is a registered trademark of American Sports Licensing, LLC
Intel® is a registered trademark of the Intel Corporation
Chevron® is a registered trademark of Chevron Intellectual Property LLC
Costco® is a registered trademark of Costco Wholesale Membership, Inc
Zappos.com® is a registered trademark of Zappos IP LLC
Gucci® is a registered trademark of Gucci America, Inc
Chick-fil-A® is a registered trademark of CFA Properties, Inc.
Twitter® is a registered trademark of Twitter, Inc

This book contains a number of photos with various business names in them, and the use of these company names is not to indicate sponsorship or endorsement of this book by these companies. These company images are being used solely for educational comment purposes under the "Fair Use Doctrine" permitted by Section 107 of the Copyright Act of 1976, where allowance is made for fair use for purposes such as criticism, comment, news reporting, teaching, scholarship, education, and research. Permission to use the photos was granted by various photographers through a stock photo image company.

ISBN-13: 978-1-957651-99-6
Library of Congress Control Number: 2024924067

Designed by *the*BookDesigners

INDIE BOOKS INTERNATIONAL®, INC.
2511 WOODLANDS WAY
OCEANSIDE, CA 92054
www.indiebooksintl.com

Dedicated to my mom.
Thank you for always reminding me
to do great things.

CONTENTS

Foreword 1

Preface 3

Part I
Why Purpose Is The New Competitive Edge 7

Chapter 1: Choose Purpose Or Choose Irrelevancy . . 9

Chapter 2: Respond To Massive Change By
Operationalizing Purpose 19

Chapter 3: Where We Are Headed 31

Chapter 4: Cracking The Code Of Purpose 35

Part II
Slaying Irrelevancy With Purpose 45

Chapter 5: Discovering What Makes Purpose
So Powerful, Before It's Too Late 47

Chapter 6: Purpose And The Human 53

Chapter 7: Knowing The Difference Between
What And Why 57

Chapter 8: How To Think Purpose Driven 65

Chapter 9: Understanding Profit Versus Purpose . . 73

Chapter 10: Setting A Baseline 77

Chapter 11: Ascending The
Value-To-Action Pyramid 79

Chapter 12: How To Become A Purpose-
Driven Company. 83

Chapter 13: Cocreating Your Purpose Statement. . 97

Chapter 14: Operationalizing Purpose 109

Chapter 15: On The Intersection Of
Purpose And Marketing. 119

Chapter 16: Knowing What A Purpose-Driven
Organization Is Not 125

Chapter 17: Purpose And The Innovation
Adoption Curve. 131

Part III

Living With Purpose 143

Chapter 18: Preparing For Growth 145

Chapter 19: Beware The Dilution Of Purpose 147

Chapter 20: Embracing Purpose—The Global
Future Of Business. 153

Appendix 157

Acknowledgments 159

About The Author 160

Purpose Workshops. 162

Works Cited And Author's Comments 165

FOREWORD

I have long been fascinated by the concept of purpose. Like the lives of so many, my life has been a twisty-turvy road filled with more questions than answers. Since first reading *A Purpose Driven Life* by Rick Warren in my early twenties, I have sought to understand my own existence and impact on the world around me.

Until fairly recently, purpose was a pursuit in my personal life. It was a topic I debated mostly in my own head and rarely shared beyond the most intimate circles. I connected purpose to family, to church, or to community. I carried on this way for over two decades, separating my thoughts about purpose from my thoughts about my career and professional aspirations.

Then, as luck would have it, I met Colt Briner. There are times when someone enters your life, and you know instantly that they are going to be important, but you rarely know in what way. What began as an easy conversation with a lot of laughs very quickly turned into vulnerable and existential conversations. Colt challenged me to think differently in a playful and gentle way. He actively listened and responded in ways that took the conversation to new and deeper planes. Before long, we had a regular commentary going about purpose over glasses of wine, on a hike, or in each other's kitchens.

Colt's concept of a purpose-driven business changed how I think about my own purpose. Instead of seeing two halves (one personal and one professional), I began to see my purpose holistically and connected deeply to the organization I was working in at the time. I saw others, at every level, come to the same conclusions and show up for work with a renewed energy focused on the greater good.

Now, it seems that more and more people are seeking this connection with their organizations. We are asking ourselves how we connect to an organization's mission before deciding to accept job offers. We want to know what an organization stands for, what it is all about, and what impact it intends to make in the world. Simply put, we want to connect with something bigger than ourselves.

Purpose and profits are not mutually exclusive. Let your organization be a beacon of light, a place where people can feel a sense of belonging, and watch how that kind of culture will impact your bottom line.

Sarah Armstrong
CEO of Trend Health Partners

PREFACE

I grew up just outside of Seattle, Washington, raised by a single mom and occasionally tormented by my older brother (we get along great now, but it was full-on *Wonder Years* back in the day). I have lots of great memories from back then—it was the before-cell-phone, "be home by dark" era—but one image above all has remained etched in my mind in the decades since a handwritten note from my mom on the inside of the front door:

Do great things.

In addition to seeing this note several times a day, the encouragement was further reinforced by my mom calling out, "Do great things," each time I left the house (even with my friends in tow).

The reactions I had to both the note and the daily rallying cry spanned everything from classic teenage eye-rolling apathy to chest-puffing determination to feeling downright intimidated. Ultimately, they served their intended purpose in motivating me to do my best in the many activities I pursued.

If you allowed me three words to sum up this book, those would be the ones I would choose: do great things. That's the fundamental guidance I am giving to modern business leaders. But let me be clear: the classic measures of business greatness are not what I am talking about.

For my entire life, the "greatness" of businesses has been measured in terms of financial value. We've gone from celebrating companies worth millions to celebrating companies worth billions, and I'm sure the trillions are right around the corner. What then? Should we march on to quadrillions?

Here's the thing: I feel like we've pretty much checked the box on building value measured in dollars. It is not like a dimpled chad checking the box, but a stabbed dead center with an eight-foot harpoon checking the box.

We did it. We got there. Awesome job everyone! We have officially achieved greatness in the dollars-measured dimension of business.

So, can we move on now? Can we please set a new metric for greatness in business? Can we possibly imagine becoming as excited about, curious about, and scientific about a business's purpose as we are about its profits?

I don't mean to abandon one for the other. I'm talking about dreaming and achieving in more than a singular dimension.

I wrote this book in service to my personal purpose: to accelerate the world's transition to a new business model—one that is driven by purpose and powered by creativity. In this book, we focus on the *what*, *how*, and *why* of business that is driven by purpose. God willing, if I survive writing this book, I'll tackle the "powered by creativity" part in a subsequent work.

Simply put, purpose is fundamental. Throughout my tenure as chief marketing and communications officer at a company nestled near Cincinnati, I bore witness to the extraordinary impact of placing purpose at the forefront of a company's mission. This commitment catalyzed our growth, skyrocketing our (privately held) valuation tenfold to over $2 billion and securing a commanding 60 percent market share within a mere three-year span.

While purpose alone didn't carve this path to success, its undeniable influence has solidified my belief that it is a cornerstone in the evolving landscape of global business. This book is born from a deep-seated desire to champion the shift toward purposeful business strategies.

Let's face facts: traditional assurances tied to work, career, and business have undergone major shifts in the past generation. Employment used to have a much stronger element of long-term security—it provided a reliable path to owning a home and living the American dream, and it offered comfort in retirement—but all that has significantly eroded in the last few decades. Such changes have led to employee disengagement, talent shortages, and a sharp rise in "quiet quitting." Amid these changes, traditional notions of retirement are fading, the American dream is evolving, and the boundary between work and personal life is blurring.

It is imperative for today's leaders to recognize and respond to these transformations. Many organizations remain tethered to archaic beliefs about job satisfaction, employee engagement, and consumer behavior.

My direct experiences with the power of purpose in business have convinced me that it is the key to unlocking success in the new paradigm.

Leaders who fail to adapt will find themselves relics of a bygone era, overtaken by those who heed the call to evolve. We are in a race for relevance, and the stakes are the future of our businesses.

My aim with this book is to impart the lessons of a purpose-driven business model and offer guidance to those ready to embark on this transformative journey.

Stay relevant, stay competitive. Join me in exploring the power of purpose and its paramount role in shaping the future of business.

Do great things.

Colton Briner
Santa Rosa, California

PART I

WHY PURPOSE IS THE NEW COMPETITIVE EDGE

CHAPTER 1

Choose Purpose
Or Choose Irrelevancy

Come back with me in time to September of 2018 and the locale of Chicago.

This was when I first met the CEO of the company where I would come to learn the power of purpose. As a courtesy of anonymity, we'll call him "Kevin."

Kevin has many admirable leadership qualities. He is inspiring, astute, and a phenomenal team builder. His superpower is his ability to unite people.

Little did I know the united purpose we would soon share.

His firm, again for the sake of anonymity, we'll call it NovaRev, operates in the revenue-cycle management space.

NovaRev supports the back office of healthcare providers—hospitals, health systems, and clinics. This is all the nonclinical work that must get done so patients can get the care they need, and providers can get paid for the work that they do. Over the last several decades, these processes have become increasingly complicated in the American healthcare system, making it harder for providers to focus on patient health and more challenging for them to get paid for their work. Companies like NovaRev off load that work from the providers so that the providers don't have to spend time fighting to get paid and can instead focus on caring for their patients.

When healthcare providers have strong financial performance (sadly, this is rare in American healthcare), they become tremendously better empowered to execute their mission: ensuring the wellness and longevity of the people in the communities in which they operate. NovaRev was helping to make this possible for the providers they worked with by being good at what they do, but there was a problem.

My first move when I started as NovaRev's chief marketing and communications officer was to interview the C-suite leaders of the health systems they were supporting. Through those conversations, it became abundantly clear to me that NovaRev's team was instrumental in ensuring the health and wellness of millions of people. In my mind, it was not a stretch to say that, through the work NovaRev was doing, they were, in fact, literally saving lives. With more time and resources to spend on fine-tuning patient care, health systems partnered with NovaRev were able to expand their clinical teams, start new clinics, add equipment and imaging machines, detect disease states earlier, and intervene to prevent progression and episodic events. That is heroic stuff.

Unfortunately, the NovaRev team members did not know those stories. Their cubicles and offices were hundreds or even thousands of miles away from the health systems they supported.

The staff was tracking all the right key performance indicators (KPIs) for revenue-cycle performance and knocking it out of the park, but they had very little insight into the true impact of their work—the human lives their work was touching.

This was the missing piece. This is what takes the day-to-day from "revenue-cycle management out-sourcing" to "redefining the possible in American health care."

Kevin had built a world-class leadership team that brought a playbook for excellence in every function of the revenue cycle of American health care. It was clear that his company would create strong career opportunities for the talent it was attracting at every level. What I didn't know at the time was how much more it would mean to give that talent a role in powerfully affecting the lives of patients. What might happen if they were empowered with that ability?

I did not have the purpose playbook in my pocket when my engagement with NovaRev began. If the disconnect between cubicle and clinic hadn't become so starkly evident to me, I don't think I would have seen the path that led me to this work in purpose. Kevin's team had built a powerful machine. What I discovered was an additive to the fuel that would help to drive it to heights never seen in the industry. The internal visibility of purpose and the alignment on mission was the turbocharger.

I can say this to business leaders now: I've walked the path. Back then, I was simply confident that the marketing strategies I believed in, along with creative execution, would put a little-known company on the industry map in short order. Kevin shared my confidence in that.

As Kevin and I discussed what it would truly mean to be all-in on being purpose-driven, we could foresee potential difficulties given the nature of the disconnect between the cubicle and the clinic.

"The key will be to truly connect NovaRev employees with the noble aspects of their work, which is giving healthcare providers the resources they need to save lives and help people live longer," I said. That is the power of relevance."

The Journey Toward Purpose-Driven Powerhouse

According to *JAMA*, the Commonwealth Fund, and *U.S. News & World Report*, American health care ranks last or near last in nearly every measure of health system performance among developed nations.[1] There are a thousand answers as to why, but the most well-known axiom in health care is "no margin, no mission." When

our providers are running on razor-thin or even negative margins, they cannot deliver world-class care.
The truth of this hit me like a freight train through the
course of the conversations I had with the health-system leaders and clinical staff of NovaRev's partners.
These were the types of conversations that NovaRev's
team did not have access to. They needed to hear these
stories to understand the true impact of their work.

Once my eyes were open to this disconnect, I discovered that it was not at all unique to NovaRev, but
rather the norm in businesses in every industry. It
was like finally seeing color after being color-blind. If
you are not familiar with the "Baader-Meinhof phe-
nomenon," this is when something you've noticed or
recently learned suddenly seems to appear everywhere. That's what I was experiencing, on a scale that
had the potential to usher in a new and more powerful model of how businesses operate in the world.
This was a big deal.

Purpose became the focal point of daily meetings,
marking a transformative shift in the organizational
ethos. The company experienced explosive growth,
adding over thousand new employees annually.
Financially, NovaRev doubled, redoubled, and again
redoubled their valuation in the span of thirty months,
attracting 60 percent market share in the US.

While a more detailed exploration of NovaRev's
experience is undertaken later in the book, it is evident
that the company thrives under a purpose-driven model.

As it maintains its trajectory of growth and prosperity, the unwavering commitment to purpose remains at the core of its success.

The NovaRev narrative serves as a testament to the potency of being a purpose-driven company, with individuals and investors alike betting on its continued triumph.

A Path To Your Purpose-Driven Future

The renowned anthropologist Margaret Mead is reported to have famously said, "Never doubt that a small group of thoughtful, committed citizens can change the world; indeed, it's the only thing that ever has."

Some critics will say being purpose-driven is pie-in-the-sky thinking, kumbaya garbage, and a waste of time and resources. In reality, the data tells a different story:

- *Employee attraction and retention.* Millennials who have a strong connection to the purpose of their organization are 5.3 times more likely to stay.[2]

- *Shareholder return.* Nearly every company with a purpose strongly embedded within the organization has a ten-year total shareholder return above the S&P 500 median.[3]

- *Marketing and sales.* Nielsen data shows a more than fourteen times higher growth rate for products with sustainability/social benefits

versus conventional products (5.8 percent
versus 0.4 percent, respectively).[4]

- *Defense from disruption.* Companies that operate
from purpose do a better job of predicting the
future, innovating in the present, and learning
from the past.[5]

In today's business world, a purpose-driven organization tackles challenges with a focus on a future vision that goes beyond specific technologies, fostering a collective aspiration.

That collective aspiration drives improved performance in nearly every measurable aspect of business performance, from product design and decision-making to customer support and revenue growth.

Perhaps you are familiar with the anecdote of the three bricklayers, an authentic parable rooted in a story. After the great fire of 1666 leveled London, the world's most famous architect, Christopher Wren, was commissioned to rebuild St. Paul's Cathedral.[6]

One day in 1671, Wren observed three hard-working bricklayers. To the first bricklayer, Wren asked, "What are you doing?"

The bricklayer replied, "I'm a bricklayer. I'm working hard, laying bricks to feed my family."

The second bricklayer responded, "I'm a builder. I'm building a wall."

But the third bricklayer, when asked the question, "What are you doing?" replied with a gleam in his eye.

"I'm a cathedral builder," he said. "I'm building a great cathedral to The Almighty."

The benefits for purpose-driven companies are plentiful, including enhanced talent attraction, increased customer loyalty, strengthened innovation capabilities, resonant marketing, augmented sales, reduced vulnerability to disruptions, increased shareholder value, and improved resilience in economic cycles.

However, realizing these advantages depends on the authenticity of a company's purpose. Organizations that merely pay lip service to purpose, substituting it with superficial statements, risk negative consequences like customer loss, talent attrition, revenue decline, and increased susceptibility to disruption by genuinely purpose-driven competitors.

Top talent increasingly seeks meaningful work, as indicated by a Deloitte survey showing that 62 percent of employees consider an organization's purpose before joining, with 36 percent ranking purpose equally crucial as salary and benefits.[7]

Great Place to Work further reinforces the tangible benefits of purpose-driven companies with data showing that such organizations exhibit higher employee retention, pride in workplace association, long-term commitment, eagerness to work, and traits linked to innovation.[8]

The findings underscore the comprehensive benefits of integrating purpose into organizational frameworks, influencing employee engagement, financial performance, consumer preference, and resilience against disruptions. Purpose-driven strategies position organizations for sustained success in today's dynamic business landscape. Purpose-driven companies outperform non-purpose-driven counterparts during challenging times, using the purpose to turn adversity into sustainable, inclusive growth opportunities.

Summing It Up

Embracing a purpose-driven approach is far from being simply idealistic; it's a strategic imperative grounded in data. When purpose permeates an organization, it has the potential to attract and retain a dedicated workforce, drive shareholder returns, stimulate market growth, and provide a robust defense against disruption. The evidence is clear: companies with a deeply embedded purpose experience remarkable advantages in every facet of their operations.

From attracting talent who are over five times more likely to stay to outperforming the S&P 500 to achieving substantially higher growth rates for purpose-aligned products, the case for purpose is compelling.

Purpose is not a nice-to-have thing—it's the cornerstone of a resilient, innovative, and future-fit business.

Next, we examine the accelerating forces of change, and the role purpose plays in helping companies navigate the escalating storm.

CHAPTER 2

Respond To Massive Change By Operationalizing Purpose

Discussing the role of purpose in business first requires an examination of the rapidly accelerating forces of change affecting nearly every aspect of modern business.

Let's glance at three startling statistics involving the Fortune 500:

- *Shapeshifting and disappearing acts.* Fortune 500 companies have been shapeshifting since the early 2000s, with more than half of them either folding, getting a new owner, or pulling a vanishing act. The drama does not stop there; another 40 percent of the survivors are predicted to commit the disappearing act within the next decade.[9]

- *Life expectancy plummets.* The average lifespan of a Fortune 500 company has dropped to roughly fifteen years in the last century. Just fifty years ago, the average lifespan was seventy-five years.[10]

- *Job-hopping doubles.* Fast forward to 2022, when 50 million folks opted to change jobs. The voluntary job-hopping doubled between 2011 and 2021, and a whopping 56 percent of American workers began eyeing new opportunities. Gallup's 2023 State of the Global Workplace Report indicated that the number remained higher than 50 percent in 2023. Meanwhile, the global start-up party is in full swing, with 305 million new start-ups—double the number from 2010.[11]

Buckle up because the speedometer of change is off the charts. The upcoming decade from 2024 to 2033 is gearing up to match the transformative roller coaster ride of the last forty years.

So, what is fueling this cresting wave of change? Two powerhouses: exponential technologies and unparalleled access.

As I write this book in 2024, 5.19 billion people will have Internet access, opening the floodgates to knowledge, talent, funding, and a whole new market vibe. It used to be that only megacompanies could afford large-scale industrial equipment, but now an average Joe can rent time on a computer numerical control (CNC) machine by the hour. We have micro-manufacturing shops that will turn out small runs of products at one one-thousandth the overhead costs of building a production facility. Do you have an idea but can't afford a chemical engineer to formulate your product? The gig economy gives anyone access to the world's top talent at highly competitive rates. Snagging million-dollar talent for short-term gigs is not a rarity; it's the new normal.

The classic barriers to entry have been rendered moot. Every individual is now massively empowered. The question becomes: why join a company at all? The answer driving the next generation of talent is the impact we can have.

But amid all the huge sea changes, some things stay constant, like the classic worries that keep business leaders tossing and turning at night. These include attracting and holding on to top talent, encouraging customer loyalty, cooking up fresh ideas, playing defense against disruptions, raking in sales, and increasing shareholder value.

These evergreen challenges remain at the core of strategic pondering, even as change continues to accelerate.

Purpose Is The New Game Changer

He who has a why to live for
can bear almost any how.
—FRIEDRICH NIETZSCHE

Remember those game-changing revolutions in business, from electricity and telephones to robots, the

Internet, and the social media era? Each one brought with it massive shifts in the competitive landscape of every industry—defining huge swaths of winners and losers. Well, the next game changer is not going to be about another technological leap. Since massive leaps are now happening multiple times in a single decade, on the way to multiple times per year, the next game changer is about becoming equipped to navigate the leaps. It's about setting a vision so clear that disruption doesn't rock the boat. Instead, you become the disruption.

Purpose-driven businesses are unlocking a cultural revolution—the secret sauce for longevity in the business game. So, whether navigating a sea of technological marvels or braving the storms of change, having a purpose as your compass is the timeless strategy for success.

You'll find that purpose-driven companies are not only outperforming but, in many cases, significantly surpassing legacy model companies. They excel in attracting and engaging talent, innovating more effectively, and achieving superior total shareholder returns—meeting all the key performance indicators a business leader uses to gauge success.

Love statistics? Here are a few that confirm the fiscal benefits to operating a purpose-driven company:

- After tracking the financial performance of eighteen purpose-driven companies over ten years, the authors of *Firms of Endearment* noted they had an average annual return on equity of 9 percent to 13.1 percent—higher than the average S&P 500 company—and found that purposeful companies outperformed the S&P 500 by ten times.[12]

- A study conducted by the Harvard Business School observed that an increase in clarity of purpose can increase return on assets by as much as 3.89 percent annually.[13]

- Research by the authors of *Built to Last: Successful Habits of Visionary Companies* found that value- and purpose-driven organizations outperform the stock market fifteen to one.[14]

And if you still need convincing, there is the following:

- Purpose-driven brands capture more market share and grow on average three times faster than their competitors, according to Deloitte—which also reports 30 percent higher levels of innovation and 49 percent higher levels of workforce retention.[15]

- A Proaction International blog post notes that "four times more consumers are likely to buy from purpose-driven companies."[16]

- According to Gallup, if just eight out of ten Americans felt their jobs had meaning, companies could realize a 41 percent drop in absenteeism, a 50 percent drop in safety accidents, and a 30 percent increase in quality.[17]

For those who use the classic business metrics of employee retention, revenue growth, shareholder return, and the like, it's patently clear that purpose is a powerful catalyst for business success. But, for myself and a rapidly growing cadre of business leaders, there is a far more compelling reason to pursue purpose as the core driver of a company: knowing that your work has meaning.

Looking beyond the head-based, logical, and economic reasons to pursue a purpose-driven model of business, we start to recognize that there are whole dimensions of heart-based motives as well:

- *Fulfillment and passion.* Purpose-driven businesses ignite passion and fulfillment by aligning daily operations with their people's deeper values. When employees see their work contributing to a meaningful cause, it fosters pride and invigoration.

- *Legacy and impact.* Leaders who focus on a purpose-driven model aim to create a lasting impact that extends beyond their tenure. The desire to leave behind a legacy of positive change drives these leaders to consider the long-term effects of their business decisions on society and the environment. By prioritizing sustainable and ethical practices, they ensure that their business helps pave the way for a better future, making their mark not just in their industry but in the world at large.

- *Employee well-being and happiness.* A purpose-driven approach has a profound impact on employee well-being. Workers who believe in the purpose of their organization are more likely to feel a palpable sense of satisfaction with their work. This positive environment fosters better mental health and even reduces workplace stress.

- *Connection and community.* At its core, a purpose-driven business model fosters a sense of community and connection among employees, customers, and the wider community. This model builds trust and loyalty by uniting people under a shared goal that reflects their values and aspirations. These connections make the business not just a commercial entity but a central part of the community's social fabric, strengthening bonds and encouraging a collaborative spirit.

- *Resilience in adversity.* Embracing a purpose-driven approach deeply influences individuals' resilience in the face of adversity.
  When employees and leaders are connected
  to a meaningful mission, they find a personal
  sense of steadiness and motivation that transcends daily challenges and setbacks. Such personal resilience not only helps individuals navigate professional obstacles but also enriches
  their emotional and mental well-being, fostering a workplace environment where people
  are more adaptive, optimistic, and capable of
  overcoming difficulties with a positive outlook.

- *Ethical pride and integrity.* For individuals working in a purpose-driven business, the alignment
  of personal and organizational values enhances
  a sense of pride and ethical integrity. When
  one's daily tasks resonate with their core beliefs,
  there is a profound sense of personal satisfaction and moral rectitude. Such a strong ethical
  foundation empowers employees to act with
  honesty and courage, even when faced with difficult choices, reinforcing their self-respect and
  commitment to integrity. The pride that comes
  from contributing to a business that positively
  affects the world fuels a deeper motivation and
  loyalty that transcends job satisfaction, cultivating a fulfilling career and life.

- *Inspiration to others.* Purpose-driven businesses lead by example, inspiring other organizations to follow their lead. The success and fulfillment demonstrated by these companies serve as a powerful testament to the viability and bene- fits of operating with a purpose. As more busi- nesses adopt similar models, the ripple effects lead to widespread changes in corporate behavior and the global business landscape.

- *Personal growth and development.* Engaging in a purpose-driven business encourages per- sonal growth among employees and leaders. The challenges and opportunities presented by aligning business practices with a purposeful mission foster skills development, innovation, and leadership abilities. Employees who feel their personal values are reflected in their work are more likely to pursue opportunities for learning and advancement, leading to a more dynamic and capable workforce and a more fulfilling work experience.

In the modern era, simply churning out a profit has become an utterly base aim. Employers who believe their staff should feel grateful just to have a job are operating from an outmoded mentality. People have awakened to the fact that they can and should seek meaning as they look to exchange their life energy with employers. Employees and consumers alike want to be part of manifesting meaningful visions and to know that their dollars and their hours are achieving something more than a transactional exchange.

Whether on the scale of an individual life, a local community, or the world at large, companies have the power to shape the future. Those who choose to accept the responsibility to do so will usher in the next era of business—one that is driven by purpose.

Summing It Up

The axis of business competition is shifting from technological innovation to cultural revolution. The ability to adapt to rapid changes and be the disruptor rather than the disrupted hinges on the successful transition to a purpose-driven model of business. This foundational strategy equips businesses to not just survive but thrive amid the ceaseless waves of change.

A clear purpose is more than a moral compass; it's a competitive edge, transforming organizations into beacons of success in a landscape where change is the only constant.

Purpose-driven companies are consistently outshining their traditional counterparts across all metrics—from talent retention to shareholder returns to providing meaning to employees and consumers alike. They embody the agility to innovate and the vision to lead, delivering tangible financial results and intangible personal fulfillment.

CHAPTER 3

Where We Are Headed

Please indulge me in a brief nautical metaphor.

John Masefield's poem "Sea-Fever" captured the romanticism of sailing ships, "all I ask is a tall ship and a star to steer her by."[18] In the seas of modern business, purpose is that star. It keeps the ship on course by providing the vision of the future that a company is sailing toward.

With purpose as your guiding star, your organization finds direction when faced with disruptions, technological surprises, or changes in the employment landscape. Purpose is the calm voice saying, "Let's stay true to our course."

This book is divided into three parts. Part I concludes with the next chapter, which is about my experience with NovaRev and the huge difference being purpose-driven made for the organization.

Part II is about a monster problem in business: being declared irrelevant. This part of the book looks at the following ways to slay irrelevancy:

- Discovering what makes purpose so powerful before it's too late

- Purpose and the human
- Knowing the difference between what and why
- How to think purpose-driven
- Understanding profit versus purpose
- Setting a baseline
- Ascending the value-to-action pyramid
- How to become a purpose-driven company
- Cocreating your purpose statement
- Operationalizing purpose
- On the intersection of purpose and marketing
- Knowing what a purpose-driven organization is not
- Purpose and the innovation adoption curve

Part III of the book covers living purpose within an organization. Being purpose-driven is an ongoing journey, not a one-time initiative that can be crossed off the list. The book concludes with these three considerations:

- Preparing for growth
- Beware the dilution of purpose
- Embracing purpose—the global future of business

So, if you take all the steps to become a purpose-driven company, what might it look like on the "other side"? The NovaRev story that follows may provide some great inspiration. My experience with this company is where I really started to crystallize my understanding of purpose.

CHAPTER 4

Cracking The Code Of Purpose

Hopefully this story inspires you to see the significant difference a company can make when it chooses the purpose-driven route.

At NovaRev, to get the prize we sought, we had to crack the code on purpose.

As mentioned previously, NovaRev is a tech-enabled business-process outsourcing company. (As stated in the introduction, I will not use real names as a courtesy of anonymity and to ensure that readers focus on the principles and lessons of the case study.)

When they hired me as their chief marketing officer, I observed that people working in cubicles didn't have any idea what their work was ultimately producing—the outcome or the impact in the world generated by their efforts. They knew their numerical goals for the day or the week on the dry-erase board, but there was this major disconnect. And it started to become much clearer to me that this disconnect was problematic.

NovaRev's work is focused on the back office of health care. They have billers, coders, collectors, patient access reps—all the things to support hospitals and health systems in the back-office functions, the machinations of billing, coding, collecting, etc.

Over the last several decades, the processes involved with health care have become more complicated, particularly in the back office. Just the work that's required to get paid as a healthcare provider has ballooned and become enormously difficult. Companies like NovaRev off-load that work so providers can focus on care.

One of the very first things I did was take a mobile recording studio with me to interview the leaders of the health systems NovaRev was supporting. I got to hear from them what it is they're able to do when they have a high-functioning, well-performing revenue cycle. What was the point of this exercise? The stories I heard from them were touching, significant, and human-needs based—real stories of lives being affected, health being improved in communities, hospitals expanding to create better access, and more tools being provided for improving care. It was very meaningful stuff. It was purpose. But there was a stark contrast between what they were talking about and what I heard back in the office, which was about coding and denied-claims management, appeals, and other nonemotional, nonpurpose-based things. It was utterly divorced from the actual impact on people's lives, the community of the world.

We undertook a company-wide initiative to change that, to bring purpose into the work NovaRev was doing by operationalizing purpose in the company. Here's the transcript of the video we created at the beginning of the campaign that was used internally and externally:

If we want a better health system, we need to be the difference.

We are finding and fixing the problems that are dragging American health care to the bottom of the list. Tens or even hundreds of millions of dollars per year in improved financial performance for the hospitals and health systems that we support—this is what our difference looks like. The denials we overturn, the charges that we capture, the underpayments that we recover, make dollars available for providers to invest in the quality of care: new imaging machines, precision surgical robots, medicine, more beds, more training, more wheelchairs. The work that we do off-loads the burden of coding, charge capture, denials management, underpayment recovery, and fifty thousand annual payer updates so that providers can focus on care. We are here because we deeply understand the problems that are bleeding our health system of resources, and we know how to fix them. We are here because we would rather prevent the denial upstream than collect

THE RACE TO RELEVANCE

commission for overturning one downstream. That's not a job; that's a partnership with American health care. Welcome to NovaRev.

While the video made for a powerful marketing piece, we primarily used it internally to reorient how our entire organization operated and thought about what we did. This was the message we wanted the staff to understand about the work we were doing.

That's where we started. It was a major energy change inside the organization and became the new language of how we identify if we were making an impact. It went beyond the KPIs in the objectives and key results (OKRs) of denials overturned, beyond revenue collected from insurance companies. It went to:

- What's happening to the health system now that they have improved financial performance?
- Were they able to open a new clinic?
- Were they able to add a new imaging machine?
- Were they able to affect the lives of the people they serve?

We started to bring in more stories.

We did a national tour and sat down with health-system leaders to create an internal campaign that gave us the opportunity to share these stories—learning things such as how one NovaRev client converted buses into mobile clinics for communities that lacked health-care facilities. We learned about hospitals that brought in early detection imaging to identify disease states like cancer in early stages and literally save lives.

We shifted the way employees understood their work from "I just enter the codes into the computer for the bill," to "we're saving lives."

This was so much more meaningful. It was hard to overstate the impact. Every month we did an impact update report that became the new language of the organization. Each month we would feature a different health system, telling their part of the story and creating a tie-in to the work that NovaRev was doing. It wasn't just what this hospital did this month, it was what this hospital did this month because of this financial per-formance, because of NovaRev's phenomenal team. We were connecting all the dots, all the time. When we sat down in meetings, it became about the impact we had created each month. Then we could unpack that top-level goal and see what was rolling up underneath it, and how we were able to make it happen.

When you start to shift the language, you start to operate differently, putting different elements into your recruiting and performance reporting. How are you incentivizing people? How are you creating your bonus structure? What are the things you're looking to see your money, actions, and hiring go behind? Everything starts to shift when you're truly, fully oper-ationalizing purpose.

Instead of just saying, "We want better health care for people," it must happen at ground level. This is how you start to see people shifting what they say whether it's to family or friends or at the bar, when asked, "What do you do?" The language changes from, "Oh, I'm in healthcare financial-management out-sourcing"—where they would be asleep before you even finished the sentence—to "I make sure hospitals have the resources they need to save lives and keep people healthy." There could hardly be a bigger differ-ence between these two statements, right?

So, what do you do?
"I'm in healthcare financial management outsourcing."
Versus
"I make sure hospitals have the resources they need to save lives and keep people healthy."

We started to recognize health systems that weren't even our clients when we saw they were purpose-driven organizations leveraging strong revenue-cycle perfor-mance to improve their facilities, create better access, support bigger charity programs, and drive better health outcomes. We'd send them awards to say, we recognize you, we see what you're doing, and we think it's awesome. For NovaRev's messaging campaigns, we'd go out and listen to health-system leaders who weren't our clients because it wasn't about who we could sell to. It was about:

- Who is a part of this difference?
- Who shares this North Star?
- Who's aligned with this purpose?
- How do we, as the collective organizations of American health care, do a better job?

Of course, as you may expect, some of the companies we talked to became clients, as did many of those we sent the awards to.

Ultimately, how did NovaRev perform? I was with the company for just over two years, and during that time, we essentially earned every award that their industry had to offer. We got top workplace awards, both in their locations and in the industry as a whole. We were recognized as #1 by the third-party rating organizations in the industry and were awarded for revenue-cycle performance excellence by the industry's leading benchmarking group.

NovaRev was also the highest-rated employer in its category on both Indeed and Glassdoor.

From the perspective of brand visibility, our purpose-centered campaigns garnered more views than all the lifetime videos of every competitor in the space. That wouldn't be a miraculous thing in consumer product sectors because we regularly see companies like Nike, Dove, and Always—the list is long—speak to people in meaningful, purpose-driven ways. But in the business-to-business (B2B) spaces and in the niche space of revenue cycle, this kind of messaging was groundbreaking.

With respect to LinkedIn engagement, we had more than twice as much as the next highest competitor: 7 percent engagement compared to 3.28 percent. That's comments, likes, shares, and reposts. Plus, we generated three times more qualified leads per dollar spent compared to the prior period.

NovaRev Marketing Result

Our purpose-driven messaging campaign garnered more views than all the lifetime videos of all competitors—combined.

LinkedIn engagement = 7.02 percent compared to 3.28 percent of the next highest competitor.

Three times more qualified leads were generated per dollar spent compared to the prior period.

Over $1M in earned media ad value.

The average email click-through rate of 15.24 percent versus the industry average of 6.99 percent.

Triple the volume of qualified leads.

The firm's ultimate bottom line is that it grew to a 60 percent market share for full-outsourcing revenue-cycle contracts in the US.

People will ask, "Well, is all that because of purpose?" No, I can't say it was all because of purpose. NovaRev had strong solutions, a stellar leadership team, and exceptional staff. They had a lot of great things going but purpose took everything up a notch. It mattered to our clients, it mattered to our prospects, it mattered to our employees. It mattered to the market in general. It helped in decision-making. It attracted talent, aligned departments, and fostered passion.

How did purpose help to drive NovaRev's results?

- Purpose mattered to the market, clients, and employees.
- It helped in decision-making.
- It created passion.
- It drove innovation.
- It attracted talent.
- It fostered partnerships.
- It aligned departments.

Summing It Up

At NovaRev, we had a successful quest. In cracking the purpose code, we saw people's ability to know the right thing to do increase. Individuals gained more autonomy, and decisions happened faster. Plus, there was greater fluidity in execution as everyone was pulling in the same direction.

Understanding purpose created passion in the organization. People weren't staying after hours because they feared losing their jobs; they were staying after hours because they knew performing for these health systems would improve people's health outcomes.

Purpose drove innovation. We knew what change we were trying to create in the world. It was never about keeping up with the latest technological development; it was only about getting to the North Star. Purpose attracted talent, fostered partnerships, and aligned our departments.

In Part II of this book, let's explore how not to fall into the trap of irrelevancy.

PART II

SLAYING IRRELEVANCY WITH PURPOSE

CHAPTER 5

Discovering What Makes Purpose So Powerful, Before It's Too Late

The time has come to debunk a myth.

A recent discovery in behavioral research has revealed that incentives *actually decrease* overall performance, specifically on tasks that require complex problem-solving. Over the past thirty years, more than one hundred experimental studies have been conducted on this topic.[19]

According to *Harvard Business Review, rewards* undermine intrinsic motivation by making people feel controlled and devaluing their work—especially when tied to interesting or complicated work. "When people view their work as externally directed and unworthy, they won't approach it with a commitment to excellence."[20]

Consider this great insight from author Daniel Pink: "Rewards work well when there is a simple task, simple rules, and a clear destination; they narrow focus and concentrate the mind. Rewards prevent us from thinking broadly. However, people may become disengaged and unmotivated at work if they don't understand, or can't invest in the 'bigger picture.'"[21]

Pink points to research conducted by psychologists Harry Harlow and Edward Deci in 1971.[22] They discovered that while rewards and incentives were effective at motivating employees when performing routine tasks, they were ineffective and even counterproductive in motivating employees in complex problem-solving.

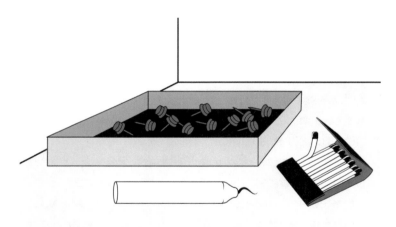

In his TED Talk, Pink refers to an experiment called the candle problem, as seen in the image above.[23] The challenge, formulated by psychologist Karl Duncker in 1945,[24] involves placing subjects in a room with a table against the wall on which a candle, a box of tacks, and a matchbook are positioned. The task is to secure the candle to the wall in such a way that it will not drip wax onto the table when lit.

Here is the solution:

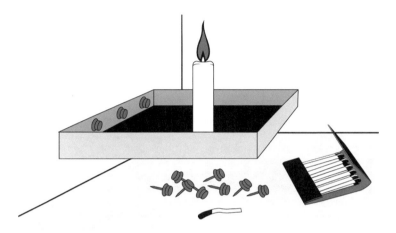

The core of the problem is functional fixedness, which refers to the limitations people place on the use of objects based on their typical uses. For instance, participants generally perceive "a box of tacks" rather than "a box and some tacks" separately, overlooking the potential alternative uses of the box, such as a candle holder.

In a follow-up experiment by Canadian professor Sam Glucksberg in 1962 at Princeton, this challenge was modified to assess the impact of financial incentives on creative problem-solving. In his setup, one group received money for solving the problem quickly, which, interestingly, delayed their solution time by an average of three-and-a-half minutes compared to those without such an incentive. Glucksberg determined that monetary rewards could inhibit creative thinking.

Glucksberg adjusted the setup in another version of the experiment by removing the tacks from the box, which improved performance in the incentivized group by simplifying the task's creative demands.[25]

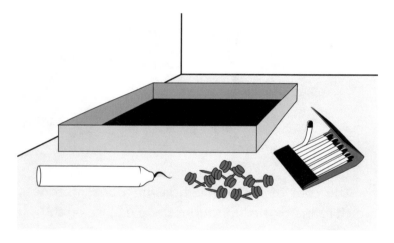

Daniel Pink refers to this adjusted version as the "Candle Problem for Dummies," suggesting that while traditional rewards can boost performance for straightforward tasks, they may hinder more complex cognitive processes. Pink advocates for intrinsic motivation—fueled by autonomy, mastery, and purpose—as more effective for engaging and motivating individuals in modern work environments.

"Those who believe that they're working toward something larger and more important than themselves are often the most hardworking, productive, and engaged. So, encouraging them to find purpose in their work—for instance, by connecting their personal goals to organizational targets using OKRs or OGSMs—can win not only their minds but also their hearts."[26]

So how does this factor into a conversation about purpose in business?

With new technologies in artificial intelligence (AI) and automation, "simple tasks" are being mechanized. Going forward, it's the complex tasks that will remain for humans to tackle. These are the very tasks that classic incentivizing doesn't work for. That's why it is so important to establish a new framework of motivation, one that doesn't counteract the intended outcome but rather supports it—one that fosters ingenuity, resourcefulness, and creative thinking. Purpose provides that framework.

Summing It Up

Purpose-driven work eclipses traditional incentives, particularly when tackling complex and higher-order-thinking tasks that remain even as technology advances. The research is clear: extrinsic rewards can impede innovative thinking, while intrinsic motivation fosters it. Glucksberg's candle problem illustrates how monetary incentives can paradoxically reduce worker performance for creative tasks. Pink's discourse on intrinsic motivation, emphasizing autonomy, mastery, and purpose, offers a blueprint for nurturing a work-force that is engaged, productive, and innovative. In the evolving landscape of work, where AI assumes routine tasks, the human capacity for complex problem-solving becomes our most valuable asset. Cultivating a purposeful workplace is more than just motivational; it's a strategic imperative for success in an increasingly complex world. Purpose is not just a lofty ideal but a practical framework for unleashing human potential and driving organizational performance.

CHAPTER 6

Purpose And The Human

L et's have a look at why purpose is so powerful from the perspective of neuroscience, and everybody's feel-good friend: dopamine.

Dopamine is a neurotransmitter, a chemical messenger that transmits signals in the brain and other areas of the body. It plays several important roles in both physical and psychological functions. Some of the key functions of dopamine include the following:

- *Reward and pleasure.* Dopamine is often referred to as the "feel-good" neurotransmitter. It's released in large quantities in response to pleasurable or rewarding experiences, reinforcing enjoyable behaviors and encouraging individuals to repeat them.

- *Motivation and desire.* Dopamine is part of the brain's reward system—it's released when we expect or receive a reward, which in turn motivates us to repeat the actions that led to the reward. This aspect of dopamine's function is integral to habit formation.

- *Cognition and attention.* Dopamine helps regulate attention and the ability to concentrate. Adequate levels of dopamine are necessary for focus and executive functions, which include planning, problem-solving, and decision-making.

Well, that all sounds lovely. So how do we keep that good stuff flowing? It turns out that you can increase your dopamine levels by setting incremental goals and making small accomplishments. In other words, the dopamine reward system engages as you make regular, incremental progress. It's not about reaching some huge climatic triumph; it's about having a sense that you're progressively moving toward something. In other other words, it is about having a purpose and steadily achieving it.

As employers, engaging the dopamine reward system as an ally is really a matter of setting the stage—establishing a purpose, clearly connecting the dots between each individual's role and that purpose, and fostering consistent visibility into how the company is achieving that purpose.

Purpose keeps the neurochemical motivators in motion. In the words of the motivational author Earl Nightingale, "Success is the progressive realization of a worthy goal or ideal." That notion of progress is reminiscent of the adage that success is a journey, not a destination. Nightingale may not have been a neuroscientist, but he did understand what makes people tick.

Speaking of knowing what makes people tick, author Simon Sinek has also made some powerful contributions to our collective understanding of what motivates people. Sinek argues that understanding and communicating the "why" behind an action or an organization's existence is the most powerful motivator. People are inspired by a sense of purpose and are more motivated when they feel they are part of something bigger than themselves. In his book *The Infinite Game*, Sinek suggests that businesses should focus on long-term goals rather than short-term gains. He argues that a mindset geared toward continuous improvement, rather than finite wins, is more motivating for teams and is more sustainable.[27]

Sinek differentiates between short-term happiness and long-term fulfillment. He suggests that true motivation comes from the latter, which is achieved through working toward something one believes in over time.

In the intricate dance of neurotransmitters that govern our brain's reward systems, purpose emerges as a potent choreographer. By harnessing the power of dopamine, the chemical embodiment of motivation and pleasure, purpose-driven actions provide a sustained release of this feel-good neurotransmitter. This steady flow keeps us engaged and propels us toward our goals, not through the pursuit of fleeting victories, but through the fulfillment derived from continuous progress. Purpose, therefore, is not just an abstract concept but a neurochemical force driving us toward achieving something greater, providing the profound satisfaction that comes with the incremental realization of a worthy ideal.

Summing It Up

Neuroscience reveals why purpose resonates so deeply: dopamine, our brain's reward messenger, thrives on the journey toward purposeful goals. Embracing an infinite mindset centered on continuous progress toward a goal emerges as a powerful motivator and sustainer for individuals and organizations alike. Employers can tap into this by connecting each role in the organization to its purpose, creating a climate where progress is visible, and the good feels keep on rolling.

Let us now turn to bridging the gap between products and services to the broader understanding of needs and purpose.

CHAPTER 7

Knowing The Difference Between What And Why

Oh, how the mighty have fallen. Do you remember going to Blockbuster to pick out a video for Friday night?

In 2000, Blockbuster was an $800 million enterprise—a titan of entertainment. But the company had a critical flaw. They believed they were in the DVD rental business. This is partially evidenced by the fact that some 16 percent of its revenues came from late fees. But the real clincher came in 2000.

In early 2000, Netflix founders Reed Hastings and Marc Randolph offered to sell their company to Blockbuster for $50 million. Blockbuster turned them down. Eventually, Netflix triumphed over Blockbuster, popularized streaming, and forced the rest of the entertainment industry to adapt.

What Netflix understood that Blockbuster did not was that it wasn't about the VHS or the DVD or delivery by mail or even streaming. It was and still is about people conveniently and affordably getting great entertainment at home and wonderful moments experienced by family and friends through entertainment.

So, let's have a look at some of the key principles that define the difference between what a company is selling and why a customer is buying.

Here's a question you may have encountered before: If a guy walks into a hardware store and asks for a quarter-inch titanium twist hex shank, what does he need? When I pose this question in my workshops, I get lots of different answers.

- One point if your answer is a drill bit.

- Ten points if your answer is a hole.

- Twenty points if your answer is to finish the project he's working on.
- One hundred points, if your answer is any one of the core needs that we all share as humans.

If we want to be effective in a new paradigm of purpose-driven business, we will need to think beyond specific products and services to the core human needs we are serving. So, let's say the project this gentleman is working on, the project he needs the drill bit for, is shelving in his garage.

Some of the core human needs being met by this individual by having the shelving in his garage are:

- harmony
- order
- beauty
- safety
- movement
- space

We call these core human needs because they are needs that are collectively shared by all humans. What happens when an individual's needs are being met? Positive feelings arise. For our shelving guy, we might expect him to have the following feelings because of his needs being met:

THE RACE TO RELEVANCE

- joy
- comfort
- relaxation
- serenity
- contentment

In his book, *This Is Marketing*, Seth Godin says:

> *The lesson is that the drill bit is merely a feature, a means to an end, but what people truly want is the hole it makes. But that doesn't go nearly far enough. No one wants a hole. What people want is the shelf that will go on the wall once they drill the hole. Actually, what they want is how they'll feel once they see how uncluttered everything is when they put their stuff on the shelf that went on the wall now that there's a quarter-inch hole. But wait… they also want the satisfaction of knowing they did it themselves. Or perhaps the increase in status they'll get when their spouse admires the work. Or the peace of mind that comes from knowing that the bedroom isn't a mess and that it feels safe and clean. People don't want to buy a quarter-inch drill bit. They want to feel safe and respected.*[28]

Let's talk about Toro. We recognize Toro as a company that builds and sells mowers, blowers, and weed whackers. But what am I really trying to get when I am buying their products?

To be correctly oriented around purpose would mean that the folks at Toro understand that serene, beautiful landscaping is what people are truly seeking when they buy from them, rather than any particular tool they sell. If Toro understands that beauty, serenity, space, and relaxation are what they're selling, and science figures out a way to manage landscaping with lasers instead of whirling blades, then it will naturally become a laser-building company. It may have completely overhauled its product line but it's still there to meet needs associated with serene landscape because it's oriented around that purpose instead of any specific product. They don't die on the hill of relentlessly innovating gas-powered mowers after the laser comes out because that was never the business they were actually in. Conversely, if they held steadfast to the idea that their company exists to continuously innovate on small-scale internal combustion engines, they will inevitably be eclipsed by a competitor that is genuinely focused on the purpose of fulfilling their customer's needs. (This is similar to when railroads evolved from being in "the train business" into the "transporting goods business.")

So, what feelings would we expect would arise in a person whose needs for beauty, serenity, space, and relaxation are being met by having a great backyard? How about joy, comfort, confidence, and pride?

Let's have a look at some common human needs that we all share. This list comes from the work of clinical psychologist Marshall Rosenburg:[29]

Universal Human Needs

This list is not complete, but it includes all nine categories and a reasonable selection of universal needs.

Connection
Acceptance
Affection
Clarity
Communication
Confirmation
Compassion
Intimacy
Understanding
Authenticity
Love

Autonomy
Choice Space
Spontaneity

Peace
Beauty
Ease
Harmony
Order
Wholeness

Interconnection
Belonging
Consideration
Community
Cooperation
Dignity
Mutuality
Support
Trust

Meaning
Contribution
Creativity
Hope
Inspiration
Purpose

Celebration
Joy
Mourning
Play

Competence
Effectiveness
Efficiency
Growth
Learning
Power

Honesty
Authenticity
Integrity

Basic Survival
Shelter
Food & Water
Rest
Safety
Security
Touch

And what are some feelings we experience when our needs are being met?

Feelings Associated with Met Needs

adventurous	glad
engaged	relaxed
loving	content
affectionate	happy
excited	satisfied
moved	curious
alive	hopeful
fascinated	tender
peaceful	delighted
calm	interested
friendly	thrilled
playful	energetic
confident	joyful
	warm

Summing It Up

This all goes back to the fact that many businesses and their employees are oriented in a very limited way due to the fact that they are not oriented around the higher dimensions of the human needs they're serving.

If you come home and your kids ask you what you do, you may say, "I make lawnmowers." It could very well be true that you're physically making lawnmowers at work, but what you're really doing is helping people to have beauty, serenity, space, and relaxation that brings them joy, comfort, confidence, and pride.

We need to bridge the gap from a limited under-standing of products and services to a broader under-standing of needs and purpose. Thinking is shifting from brand-oriented and product-oriented to pur-pose-oriented and needs-oriented thinking. The topic of how to think purpose-driven will be considered in the next chapter.

CHAPTER 8

How To Think Purpose-Driven

An easy way to get a read on how purpose-oriented someone is to ask the following question:

"What do you use Wi-Fi for at your house?"

If they say, "Netflix, Google, my Ring doorbell, my Nest thermostat, and FaceTime," they are, like most people, product-oriented.

However, if they say, "Home entertainment, knowledge and understanding, making my house comfortable, keeping my family secure, and staying connected with my loved ones," they would be among the rare but growing population of purpose-oriented thinkers.

Getting our minds to convert to a purpose orientation takes effort. We have been operating in a product-forward paradigm for so long that we need to do some unlearning before we can expect to restructure our thinking.

Let's have a look at some familiar products to see if we can kick-start the process.

Up first, Red Bull.

Red Bull is a beverage company that offers energy drinks.
PHOTO: Erik Mclean on Unsplash

What does this company sell? Yes, it's an 8.4-ounce canned beverage, but what does it represent to the consumer? What need are they generally seeking to meet when they buy this product?

Red Bull sells energy—the energy you need to accomplish your goals. It's not about flavor (I'm still not really sure what that flavor is, honestly). It's not about thirst, which frankly makes sense because caffeine, an ingredient in Red Bull, is a diuretic. It's not about nutrition (there are 26 grams of sugar in those little cans). It's about energy that empowers us to meet our needs for accomplishment, effectiveness, play, and aliveness.

Let's try another.

Polaroid develops technology products, including instant, digital still, and sports action video cameras, TVs, mobile apps, and apparel.
PHOTO: Eniko Kis on Unsplash

What is Polaroid selling? Is it a self-contained photo capture and print device or a means to preserve memories of special moments in life? We buy a Polaroid camera (yes, they are still in business) because we want to capture moments in time. Polaroid sells memories and those memories give us a method to meet our need to celebrate life, our need for joy, and our need to matter to ourselves.

Then there's this.

Rolex is a manufacturing company that designs
and manufactures watches for men and women.
PHOTO: Pio3 on DepositPhotos

What is Rolex selling? Is it a timepiece? I can meet my need for a timekeeping device with a $25 Casio. Rolex is selling status and prestige. People use that status and prestige to meet their need for attention, belonging, respect, power, and self-expression.

How about a more advanced challenge?

Shopify is a cloud-based, multi-channel commerce
platform designed for small and medium-sized businesses.
PHOTO: Monticello on DepositPhotos

What does Shopify sell? A digital storefront? Payment processing solutions? The answer is entrepreneurship, and the needs they are meeting are self-actualization and personal achievement.

Now for an important distinction: needs versus preferences versus methods.

One area where people run into trouble is not understanding the difference between needs, preferences, and methods.

Let's take a look at a hypothetical example in what I call the pink pencil story.

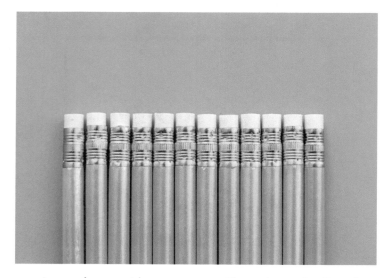

A couple are at home on an otherwise quiet Sunday, but the wife is quite distraught. She's basically on a rampage throughout the house to find her pink pencils. She has been through every cabinet, every drawer, every shelf, and even the couch cushions. She's all over the house. Her husband has clearly heard her declare that she is desperately trying to find her pink pencils, but he isn't engaged whatsoever.

Essentially, he perceives her behavior as irrational. He can't wrap his mind around pencils causing the level of angst he is observing in his wife. The reality is that there are key human needs at play here, needs that he would easily relate to, but there are two points of disconnect that have obscured them: preference and method. The actual core human need at play for the wife is self-expression—a need the husband knows, understands, and shares. Indeed, it is a need we all share and we have different methods that we employ to meet. The method that the wife in our story employs to meet her need for self-expression is journaling. And when she journals, her preference, from all the way back to elementary school, is to use pink pencils.

Now if the husband understood that the absence of the pink pencils represents an obstacle for her in getting a core human need met, he would be much more likely to engage, or at least not think she's crazy for stressing about pencils. Scrambling around the house to find pencils for your spouse when there are perfectly good pens readily available might seem like a waste of time, but helping a spouse in getting a core need met holds a whole different meaning.

We all have preferences within the methods we employ when we seek to get our needs met, and expressing oneself is a human need we can all understand. You may not personally employ the method of journaling, nor may it be that the color of pencil you use is of much concern to you, but the more you look for the core human needs behind people's methods and preferences, the better you can understand the behaviors of those around you. Ultimately, this will help you on your way to becoming a purpose-driven thinker.

Summing It Up

It's crucial to recognize that the transition from a prod-uct-centric to a purpose-driven mindset is a transfor-mative process, one that redefines our understanding of what we sell and why. Looking through the lens of everyday items, from Red Bull to Rolex, we see that the essence of what's being sold goes beyond the tangible product—it's the intangible aspirations like energy, memories, status, or entrepreneurial spirit that truly resonate with consumers. Grasping this concept is key to becoming purpose-driven. It involves seeing past the immediate utility to the core human needs behind consumer choices, a perspective shift that not only enhances business acumen but also enriches our engagement with the world around us. By fostering this understanding, leaders can inspire more meaning-ful connections, foster stronger innovation, and create products that embody the very essence of purpose.

CHAPTER 9

Understanding Profit Versus Purpose

In *Start with Why*, author Simon Sinek discusses the perils of playing the price game, noting that it's all too easy for companies to fall into a downward spiral of price addiction. Sinek writes, "Price always costs something. The question is, how much are you willing to pay for the money you make?"[30]

> *Profit isn't a purpose, it's a result.*
> —SIMON SINEK

Beware: Purpose For Profit Can Backfire

If a company wants purpose because it thinks it will bring them profits, then beware. If they want to put purpose up on the wall and promote it in their marketing but haven't operationalized it and don't intend to, it's going to backfire horribly. When purpose becomes platitude, it hurts, and it hurts bad.

A truly operationalized purpose attracts talent. It attracts customers. It protects a company from disruption. But business leaders who just want to get the perks without actually orienting their efforts around a genuine purpose will soon see employee turnover, client churn, and lost market share. Hence the double-edged sword of purpose.

That's it! Do you want to run a company focused solely on profits at any cost or be at the helm of an organization that has a deeper purpose—which, if authentic, will outpace profit-driven competitors in the long run?

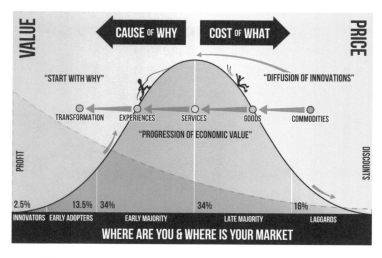

This graphic, based on work by The Inking Canvas, illustrates the point. Of note is the difference between commodity goods and transformational offerings. Value, as gauged in the minds of consumers, is highest on the left side—where purpose-oriented (transformation-focused) companies and solutions reside. The further you get from solutions that are driven by purpose (moving left to right), the more price becomes a factor.

Takeaway: either come with purpose or come with discounts.

I bring this up to focus on how important it is to shift your mentality from a profit focus to a purpose focus. The irony, of course, is that focusing on purpose has been proven to drive better financial performance, as noted in the previous chapters. Making the mentality shift isn't just a CEO thing. To truly operationalize purpose, it needs to happen for every role in every department. Here are some examples across several core business functions:

Profit Focused

Sales Narrative	Marketing Messaging	Leadership	Customer Service	Operations	Product Management
I need to meet my quota. I'm here to close the deal.	I need to get the attention of potential customers.	We need to improve the bottom line.	I help customers solve problems.	I enable our business to function.	I stock products with the highest margin.

Purpose Focused

Sales Narrative	Marketing Messaging	Leadership	Customer Service	Operations	Product Management
I am here to add value. Customer-impact is our end game.	I want to show customers how their lives will be different for business with us.	We need to deliver better results for our clients.	I help our customers be successful.	I improve our clients' businesses and lives.	I stock products that are best at solving our clients' problems.

Looking at the sales role as an example, a profit-focused sales narrative would be, "I need to meet my quota. I'm here to close the deal." On the surface, that sounds like a perfectly reasonable salesperson's charter, but that's because we've been so classically conditioned on the profit motive. Once you hear the purpose-focused sales charter—"I'm here to add value. Customer impact is our end game,"—the difference and the advantage are obvious.

Summing It Up

The interplay between profit and purpose can be a slippery slope. This is especially true in highly commoditized markets. When you compare money-oriented versus purpose-oriented, you start to see where you'd end up in this battle: race to the bottom on price or race to relevance in the mind of the customer.

Profits result from effectively operationalizing purpose, but when purpose becomes platitude or is pursued as a tactic to drive profits, it will undermine every measure of business performance. Either wield it true or not at all.

In the next chapter, we look at how to measure the degree to which a company is, or isn't, genuinely purpose-driven.

CHAPTER 10

Setting A Baseline

With this book, my primary aim is to guide leadership teams in transitioning their companies to sustainable, purpose-driven models. As with any transformative journey, we need to be able to measure our success and, for that, need to establish a baseline. While purpose may seem purely qualitative, it's actually possible to quantify how well a company is doing. I use the following survey to gauge the current degree of purpose-driven orientation and operationalization within a company. I like to get this survey sent out to staff well before any meetings, workshops, or company announcements to get a pure read on where they actually stand. I typically repeat the survey twelve months after the company begins its journey to purpose to see how well they are coming along.

Purpose Driven Self Assessment

0% --- 10% --- 20% --- 30% --- 40% --- 50% --- 60% --- 70% --- 80% --- 90% --- 100%

In your dreams   On a good day   Nailed it

- ☐ Our company serves a clear visionary purpose with present-day relevance
- ☐ Our employees keenly understand how their work serves that purpose
- ☐ Our purpose inspires and motivates our employees
- ☐ Our leaders understand the benefits of being purpose driven as a company
- ☐ Our customers see their patronage as a means to participate in and support our purpose
- ☐ Our business objectives, goals and measures are tied to our purpose
- ☐ Our strategic decisions are guided by our purpose
- ☐ Our innovation efforts are guided by our purpose
- ☐ We are achieving our purpose
- ☐ Our purpose differentiates us from others in the market

Once a baseline is set, the next phase involves cocreating the company's purpose and crystalizing it with a clear statement. After that, the real challenge, where most companies fail, lies in operationalizing that purpose—translating it into strategies and concrete actions.

Next, we take a look at the first step on the actual journey to purpose: transforming value into vision.

CHAPTER 11

Ascending The Value-To-Action Pyramid

A company's purpose is, first and foremost, derived from its values. In this case, "values" refer to what you stand for, what you believe in, and what you hold in high regard. Your values are based on the future you seek to create and the purpose you set; this goes for both businesses and individuals.

After purpose comes mission: What are you doing to achieve it? What products do you build? What services do you provide?

And then comes strategy: how are you going to go about it? What steps are taking take to reach your desired goal?

At the very top of the pyramid are your specific actions and success metrics: Who will do what? How will you measure your results? George is going to handle this. Amanda's going to take care of that. You're going to use this KPI here, that OKR over there, etc.

After laying out the theory, principles, and data around purpose-driven business, the first exercise business leaders are taken through in my workshop focuses on defining the company's values.

The team is prompted with the following questions:

- What does our company value and believe in?
- Why does our company exist?
- What is our company aspiring to be?
- What is our company uniquely great at?
- What inspires me personally to work here?

I give them three minutes to each write out as many one-word responses as come to mind while they think about these questions. Sometimes, in the last sixty seconds, I will help them along by bringing up a list of values to draw from.

Accountability	Belonging	Contentment
Achievement	Career	Contribution
Adaptability	Caring	Cooperation
Adventure	Collaboration	Courage
Altruism	Commitment	Creativity
Ambition	Community	Curiosity
Authenticity	Compassion	Dignity
Balance	Competence	Diversity
Beauty	Confidence	Environment
Being the best	Connection	Efficiency

Equality	Job security	Safety
Ethics	Joy	Security
Excellence	Justice	Self-discipline
Fairness	Kindness	Self-expression
Faith	Knowledge	Self-respect
Family	Leadership	Serenity Service
Financial stability	Learning	Simplicity
Forgiveness	Legacy	Spirituality
Freedom	Leisure	Sportsmanship
Friendship	Love	Stewardship
Fun	Loyalty	Success
Future generations	Making a difference	Teamwork
Generosity Giving back	Nature	Thrift
Grace	Openness Optimism	Time
Gratitude	Order	Tradition
Growth	Parenting	Travel
Harmony	Patience	Trust
Health	Patriotism	Truth
Home	Peace	Understanding
Honesty	Perseverance	Uniqueness
Hope	Personal fulfillment	Usefulness
Humility	Power	Vision
Humor	Pride	Vulnerability
Inclusion	Recognition Reliability	Wealth
Independence	Resourcefulness	Well-being
Initiative	Respect	Wholeheartedness
Integrity	Responsibility	Wisdom
Intuition	Risk -taking	

While this exercise is typically run in a workshop context with leadership teams, it's important to keep in mind that shifting a company to a purpose-driven model is an everyone-at-every-level endeavor. The more you can engage, enroll, and hear from your "front line," the better. After all, they are the operators of your purpose, the ones who put the rubber on the road. If you have the opportunity to run these exercises company-wide, I highly recommend that you do so.

After everyone has written out their responses, we then go through a tallying process. It goes as follows:

1. First, create four columns on a whiteboard, labeling them 1X, 2X, 3X, and 4X+.

2. Select a person to go first, calling out their first word. Those who have that same identical word all raise their hands.

3. Write the word in the box that corresponds to the number of people who had that word.

4. Each person then circles that word on their own sheet to mark that it has been tallied.

5. The first person continues calling out all their remaining words, and the scribe enters the words into the appropriate boxes.

6. The next person calls out their remaining uncircled words, which the scribe enters into the appropriate boxes.

7. Continue until everyone has called out their remaining uncircled words and entered them in the appropriate boxes.

Following the tally process, open a brief discussion to ensure everyone is satisfied that the words captured in the 4X+ column accurately represent the collectively shared values of the team/company. Allow cases to be made for changes until you reach satisfaction.

Next let's look at how to go from knowing your values to defining purpose and crafting a powerful purpose statement that people can rally around.

CHAPTER 12

How To Become
A Purpose-Driven Company

Transforming into a purpose-driven organization takes time, but there's a blueprint to follow to get there:

1. Cocreate - The company's visionary purpose

2. Communicate - The purpose throughout the organization

3. Integrate - The purpose into every function of the business

4. Share - The stories of that purpose manifesting in the world

5. Track and measure - The organization's progress through the lens of purpose

6. Build trust - By living out purpose at every level in the organization

We've learned why purpose matters and the potential results of effectively operationalizing it (or failing to). Now let's shift to the nuts and bolts of getting it done.

First on the roadmap is cocreating a powerful purpose statement. We'll begin by looking at the purpose statements of some well-known companies.

Can you guess which company each of these statements belongs to?

1.

To organize the world's information and
make it universally accessible and useful.

2.

To fulfill dreams of personal,
All-American freedom

3.

To empower every person and organization
on the planet to achieve more.

4.

To create happiness for people of
all ages, everywhere.

1.

Google is a multinational corporation that specializes in Internet-related services and organizes the world's information.
PHOTO: Adarsh Chauhan on Unsplash

2.

Harley-Davidson manufactures motorcycles.
PHOTO: Harley Davidson on Unsplash

3.

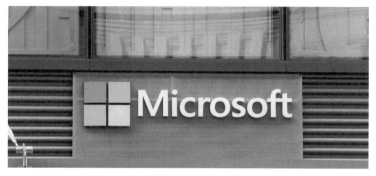

Microsoft is a software corporation that develops,
manufactures, licenses, supports, and sells a
range of software products and services.
PHOTO: Robert K. Chin

4.

Disney is a multinational mass media and entertainment conglomerate
that offers movies, shows, e-commerce, and parks to global audience.
PHOTO: Robert Way on Shutterstock

5.

To give people the power to share and make
the world more open and connected.

6.

To accelerate the world's transition
to sustainable energy.

7.

To refresh the world and inspire moments
of optimism and happiness

8.

Build the best product, cause no unnecessary
harm, use business to inspire and implement solutions to the environmental crisis.

5.

Facebook AI offers technology and engineering services like theory,
algorithms, applications, software and hardware infrastructure.
PHOTO: Greg Bulla on Unsplash

6.

Tesla Motors is an electric vehicle and clean energy company that
provides electric cars, solar, and renewable energy solutions.
PHOTO: Tesla Fans Schweiz on Unsplash

7.

Coca-Cola Enterprises is a marketer, producer, and distributor of non-alcoholic drinks. PHOTO: EasyLife Designs on Unsplash

8.

Patagonia's values reflect those of a business started by a band of climbers and surfers, and the minimalist style they promoted. PHOTO: Tim Foster on Unsplash

A purpose statement speaks to what your company seeks to achieve—what impact it seeks to create in the world. Questions to ask during the process of drafting your purpose statement include:

- Why does our company exist?
- How is the world better because of the work that we do?
- What was the mission and vision of our founders?
- If you had to describe to a child why our work matters, what would you say?
- What achievements have defined our company?

- What core human needs do we believe our customers are able to meet because of the work that we do?
- What impact would you say we had upon the world over the last twelve months?
- What would render our work moot to the world?

A purpose statement functions as the company's North Star. It will help to elucidate decisions at every level: the things you'll do, the things you won't do, how you'll do them, who you'll hire, what markets you'll enter, what solutions you will develop.

What a Purpose Statement is For:

- Speaks to the impact a company seeks to create

- Sets a company's north star

- Attracts people who value/seek that change, want to be a part of it

- Answers the question: why am I spending my life energy here

In addition to hitting those marks, you want to ensure your purpose statement checks all the boxes on the left (effective) side below, rather than straying into the right (ineffective) side.

Drafting Purpose Statements

An Effective Purpose Statement	An Ineffective Purpose Statement
Uses language your constituents use	Uses jargon, doesn't understand your audience
Is emotionally stirring	Is logical and cold
Communicates the "why"	Communicates only the "what" or "how"
Is concise	Is really long
Is a single powerful sentence	Is a rambling paragraph
Sounds good spoken out loud	Is full of clauses and hard to say
Is memorable	Is forgettable
Surprises	Is dull
Is actionable	Can't be quantified
Is specific	Is vague

And now for the cheat code: to keep things simple, format your purpose statement as a target, an action, and a result—who you are serving, through what means, and toward what end. Observe the following examples.

Allstate: We help customers realize their hopes and dreams by providing the best products and services to protect them from life's uncertainties and prepare them for the future.

Target: Customers

Action: Protect them from life's uncertainties and prepare them for the future

Result: Realize their hopes and dreams

Dick's Sporting Goods: We create confidence and excitement by inspiring, supporting, and personally equipping all athletes to achieve their dreams.

Target: All athletes

Action: Equipping them to achieve their dreams

Result: Creating confidence and excitement

Intel: We create world-changing technology that enriches the lives of every person on the planet.

Target: Every person on the planet

Action: Create world-changing technology

Result: Enriching lives

And here's my company's purpose statement:

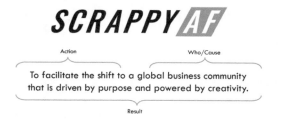

SCRAPPY AF

Action — Who/Cause

To facilitate the shift to a global business community that is driven by purpose and powered by creativity.

Result

SCRAPPY AF

Summing It Up

Creating a purpose statement your team can rally around is a critical step toward becoming a purpose-driven company. As you create your own purpose statement, remember what it's for:

- Speaking to the impact you wish to create

- Setting your North Star
- Attracting people who value/seek that change—and want to be part of it

In the next chapter we'll learn how to cocreate a purpose statement as a team.

CHAPTER 13

Cocreating Your Purpose Statement

E nough with the theory. Let's create!

While it is certainly an option to have a company's purpose statement drafted by the singular hand of the CEO (preferably with a ton of frontline input), I have found that cocreated purpose statements do a better job of fostering ownership and accountability as well as instilling excitement and energy in participants. So, while I typically conduct this exercise in the context of executive workshops, purpose-statement crafting is a great opportunity to build buy-in by enrolling all levels of an organization in the process.

Here's how it works.

Each participant will serve as both creator and judge, drafting their own statements and evaluating the statements drafted by others. The three statements that garner the highest scores will be put through a second round of judging and editing until a final, singular statement emerges.

Do not strive for more than 80 percent delight. Purpose statements are a form of art, and as with all forms of art, they are subjective in nature. Striving for 100 percent of your team to be 100 percent delighted with your purpose statement can/will lead to a much more protracted process and can even erode morale.

Before attempting to draft statements for your company, I recommend a little practice first.

Have your team consider the following companies one at a time and take a stab at creating their own target-action-result statement for each of them. Let them call out their ideas. It's not about guessing the actual purpose statements these companies have published. It's about reflecting on what you have gleaned from these brands over the decades that you've known them and distilling it into a single statement—exactly what you are going to attempt with your own brand right after this little practice round.

Chevron Corporation is an integrated energy and technology
company. Photo: Luis Ramirez on Unsplash

Whole Foods Market is a supermarket chain owned by Amazon
that exclusively sells natural and organic products.
PHOTO: Karsten Winegeart on Unsplash

Costco is a membership-only warehouse club that
provides a wide selection of merchandise.
PHOTO: Marcus Reubenstein on Unsplash

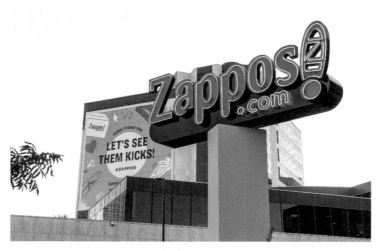

Zappos.com is an online retailer known primarily for its wide selection
of shoes, but it also sells clothing, accessories, and home goods.
PHOTO: Zappos.com press page

Gucci is a luxury brand known for Italian-style
high fashion with traditional craftsmanship.
PHOTO: Green Liu on Unsplash

Chick-fil-A is a fast food restaurant company that serves chicken
sandwiches and burgers using buns along with coffee and other
beverages. PHOTO: Brad on Unsplash

At this point, many people can't resist looking up the actual statements from these companies to see how close they got. Go ahead if you must, but remember the point is practicing the formula, not divining the actual statements these companies have published.

Now, we're ready to craft and evaluate statements for your company. Some teams will hammer this out in an hour; some will take days. Either way, each member of the team should craft and submit their best take at articulating your company's purpose. Some will eschew the formula altogether, and that's perfectly fine—it's there to provide a template for those who prefer some structure.

Once all the statements have been submitted, it's time to narrow down the field.

So how does one evaluate a purpose statement? An ideal purpose statement meets all the following criteria:

- *Value-based.* Speaks to the *why*—what we value and believe in.
- *Instructional.* Can be used as a North Star to guide thought, decision, and action.
- *Appealing.* Well crafted and sounds good.
- *Aspirational.* Relates to a desirable future state.
- *Unique.* Points to what we are uniquely great at.
- *Achievable.* Measurable and within the bounds of what the organization can accomplish.

- *Inspiring.* Creates an emotional impact, motivates staff, and attracts talent.
- *Shared.* Reflects the common vision of the leadership team.

Again, we're not looking for ten out of ten for each criterion. These are just guidelines to help your team with the process.

Now that you have a stack of statements from your team and some criteria to judge them by, it's time for your team to vote.

Oh, how I choose thee, let me count the ways.

There are many different ways for a team of people to reach a singular selection. Here are just a few of them.

- *Majority vote*: This is the simplest and most common method. Each member of the team casts a single vote, and the statement with the most votes wins. This method is effective for quick decisions but might not always reflect the preferences of all team members.

- *Consensus*: This method involves discussion and negotiation until all team members agree on a single outcome. It ensures that all viewpoints are considered and that everyone supports the final decision, although reaching a consensus can be time-consuming.

- *Ranked choice voting*: In this method, team members rank their preferences among several options. Votes are tallied in rounds, with the least popular option eliminated in successive rounds until one option has a majority. This method helps to ensure that the final choice is acceptable to a broader section of the group.

- *Dot voting*: Each team member is given a set number of dots or stickers, which they can allocate among different options. They can place all the dots on one option or spread them out. The option with the most dots at the end wins. This method is particularly useful for visualizing group preferences.

- *Single transferable vote* (STV): Like ranked-choice voting, STV allows members to rank their preferences. If no option wins an outright majority, the least popular option is eliminated, and votes are transferred based on second preferences, and so on, until one option achieves a majority. This method is particularly effective for larger groups.

- *Veto voting*: Each member has the chance to veto options. The options with the fewest vetoes proceed to the next round of consideration until only one option remains. This method ensures that the final decision is tolerable to all members, although it may not be everyone's top choice.

Personally, I like ranked choice; however, when time is limited, I tend to use dot voting.

Again, you're shooting for 80 percent delight.

Also, it's not at all uncommon for statements to undergo real-time editing by the group during the voting/narrowing process, especially with the consensus and veto methods mentioned above.

So, if your team managed to avoid devolving into a *Lord of the Flies* or a *Thunderdome* situation along the way, you should now have your purpose statement.

Great job, that took a lot of work. And now...welcome to the starting line.

As we might recall from chapter 6, having a purpose statement doesn't make you purpose-driven. It gives you a star to steer toward. Being a truly purpose-driven company requires operationalizing your purpose across the departments and levels of your organization. Creating a purpose is the starting line, not the finish line. It's a marathon you're going to keep running.

Sometimes, in this process of crystalizing a company's purpose, you find some small percentage of the people who will say, "Oh, that's not what I thought we were doing here. That's not what I want to be a part of." And that's OK, they'll find something else. But those who remain will be even more engaged and energized toward that common purpose. They pour more of their talents into it. They're more committed. Great things happen when the value of purpose dawns on your people. They come to the realization that it's not about the product or service, but how that product or service helps to bring about a vision.

Summing It Up

By embracing a collaborative approach to crafting your company's purpose statement, you lay the groundwork for shared ownership and genuine engagement. Remember, perfection is not the aim. Rather, choose a statement that resonates deeply and will guide the majority's actions and decisions.

As you weave this newly minted purpose into the fabric of your organization, you might encounter divergence of thought. This is a natural part of the process. Those who align with the defined purpose will become the bedrock of your evolving company culture, driving the organization forward with renewed passion and commitment. Creating the purpose statement is merely the commencement of a continual journey toward embodying and operationalizing that purpose, marking the true genesis of a purpose-driven enterprise.

In the next chapter, we will look at how to operationalize purpose.

CHAPTER 14

Operationalizing Purpose

Now that you have cocreated your purpose, it is time to translate it into actions. This is where you operationalize your company's purpose—bake it into the organization's DNA. Ultimately, each team member will need to make clear commitments on specific actions to move your organization forward into purpose.

The best guidance I can offer on setting actions is that ownership makes all the difference. Let your team leaders craft their own action plans. This gives them a better sense of ownership, allows plans to be better aligned with their personal strengths, and capitalizes on their knowledge of their respective departments.

In a nutshell, the answer to the question, "So what should I do to operationalize purpose in my department?" is, "You tell me."

My favorite exercise for capturing action commitments is the "sticky note" exercise.

The exercise's goal is for each participant to document actions that they are committed to taking toward operationalizing purpose in their respective departments.

Here's how it works. Get your team leaders together

in a room. Make sure that you have included leaders from every department and function in your organization:

- Revenue/growth
- Client delivery/support
- Finance
- Information technology
- Executive leadership
- Human resources
- Marketing and communications
- Operations
- Research and development

Every company is different. You may have departments not listed above. Make the effort to include representation from every department.

To prepare the room for the exercise, print out signs with the names of each department and tape them to the wall. Then, provide each leader with a pad of sticky notes (ideally each in a different color).

Tell your leaders that they will be writing out specific actions that would support the operationalization of purpose in the company. In addition to actions that would apply to their own business unit, encourage them to think about actions for other departments.

Before they start writing out actions, it can be useful to provide department leaders with some "serving suggestions" to get the ideas flowing. Here are some serving suggestions that cover a broad range of departments and functions:

- *Connect the dots.* Ensure that every team member is clear on how their role ties into and supports the company's purpose.

- *Add to agendas.* Add purpose to the top of your meeting agendas, including actual measures, goals, and progress.

- *Create internal visibility.* Capture and share client impact stories internally.

- *Drive customer awareness.* Incorporate purpose-driven narratives into customer interactions, highlighting the company's commitment to making a difference.

- *Update job descriptions.* Integrate purpose into your job descriptions; describe the kind of people you're looking for—the ones who find this kind of mission and value system personally meaningful to them.

- *Include in reviews.* Integrate purpose into your department and employee reviews and evaluations. Evaluate them based on how they contribute to the organization's ultimate purpose.

- *Make KPIs count.* Educate team members on the relationship between departmental KPIs and the overall company purpose. Show how performing well in each specific measurable aspect of a role, job, or department manifests that purpose in the world.

- *Take the thought leader route.* Generate market-facing thought-leadership content to help others advance your purpose. Share tactics, best practices, strategies, and executables, so other people and organizations can do a better job at manifesting this purpose in the world.

- *Innovate for purpose, not profit.* Orient your solution development, your innovation work, etc., around your purpose rather than trying to outpace your competitors.

- *Give purpose awards internally and externally.* Give rewards and recognition to employees, clients, and even nonclients for achieving purpose. Recognize stellar performers out in the marketplace. Become an institution whose award is meaningful.

- *Create leader events.* Create summits and roundtable events for purpose-aligned industry leaders to cooperate with each other.

- *Pick purpose partners.* Seek out purpose-aligned vendors, suppliers, and partners.

- *Align your incentives.* Tie your bonus structure to the achievement of purpose.

- *Redefine brand messaging.* Focus on the company's purpose and core values, ensuring transparency and honesty in all advertising.

- *Reevaluate the product life cycle.* Align sourcing,

production, and distribution according to purpose.

- *Set expectations*. Develop a code of conduct that upholds the company's purpose.

The facilitator presents the following instructions and checks in on the individual leaders as needed during the process. The overall time for this exercise can vary, but usually takes about an hour.

1. Each leader writes ideas (one per sticky note) on how to operationalize purpose in the company. Ideas can be specific to individual departments (either their own or others) or they can be company-wide suggestions. Ideas must be actionable. The more concrete, discrete, and measurable the better. Allow fifteen to twenty minutes for this phase.

2. Have them place their ideas on the wall under the department name that each idea applies to. General, company-wide ideas can be placed outside the department areas.

3. Once the ideas have been placed, give your team time to peruse the collection. Each participant should check out the suggestions in the column they "own" as well as those in other columns—cross-pollination adds a lot to this exercise.

Once everyone has had a chance to review the full gallery of ideas, it is time to set commitments.

In the workshops that I conduct, I provide the following form for participants to capture commitments and document new perspectives on the company's collective purpose and their individual roles.

Purpose-Driven BusinessLeadership Worksheet

Name	Department

How is my role tied to the company's purpose?

How will I help to communicate our purpose and create visibility for our impact?

What new expectations will I have for my department staff?

How will I support them in meeting those expectations?

How will I help address these identified challenges?	
Enrolling team membets that may have difficulty adapting/engaging	
Executing in harmony as a leadership team as the company grows	
Effectively connecting dots between work (individually & collectively) and impact on the world	
Keeping the fire alive	

Three actions I can take between now and to support our purpose launch event			
Action	Timeframe	Success Measure(s)	Goal(s)

Three purpose related objectives I will own going forward from the launch event			
Action	Accountable to	Measures	Time Commitment

There are a couple of quick notes about this form.

First, before I conduct workshops, I interview the leaders individually to capture their preworkshop perspectives on purpose, run them through the survey from chapter 7, and capture the top challenges, obstacles, and difficulties they expect to encounter in transitioning their company to a purpose-driven operation. The identified challenges listed in the example were captured from various teams prior to their workshops. Rather than giving them my thoughts on how to address these challenges I have found it much more effective to have them revisit the challenges after they have gained the knowledge from the workshop (essentially everything in the preceding chapters). It's remarkable how easy and intuitive the answers to their previously daunting challenges become once they understand the principles and benefits of purpose-driven business.

Second, you will notice in the worksheet that pre- and post-"launch event" actions are being captured. This is for organizations that wish to undertake a company-wide kickoff event to mark the beginning of their journey to purpose. Launch events can be a powerful way to infuse energy and enroll staff across an organization. Just make sure that you couple visibility of purpose with visibility of action. Otherwise, you're just launching a platitude.

Actions and objectives should be collectively recorded in a central location that is viewable by all who participated. Going forward, these commitments should be treated in the same way as all other job roles and respon-sibilities—owned, tracked, and accounted for.

Again, in a workshop format, this is typically an exercise I conduct with an organization's depart-ment leaders, but that is by no means where commit-ment-making ends. This exercise should be repeated at every level until each employee has documented how they understand the company's purpose, how their role supports that purpose, and what they will be doing to support that purpose.

Summing It Up

Operationalizing purpose is about transforming a shared vision into tangible actions that resonate throughout an organization's operations.

It starts with ownership; leaders must craft action plans personalized to their strengths and departmen-tal knowledge.

The sticky note exercise is a practical tool for doc-umenting commitments, fostering cross-departmen-tal collaboration, and ensuring that every department contributes to the company's overarching purpose.

With a shift toward action-focused frameworks, leaders find innovative solutions to previously insur-mountable challenges, embedding purpose into the DNA of the company.

CHAPTER 15

On The Intersection Of Purpose And Marketing

While I plan to explore the topic of purpose-driven marketing in my next book, I would like to touch on it briefly here to make a point: when a company's purpose and marketing are aligned, not only can it achieve massive results as measured in the classic metrics of business, but the marketing itself will become a force for manifesting the company's purpose.

Three campaigns that had memorable results reflecting their companies' commitment to their purpose through their advertising are the following:

1. Always

PHOTO: SOPA Images Limited

The purpose statement for Always, a P&G company, is to build girls' confidence, especially during puberty. Their "Like a Girl" campaign wasn't about products, features, or benefits. It was about uplifting the self-esteem of young women—a bullseye for their purpose. Not only was their campaign effective in conveying a powerful message to young women, but it also achieved massive results in market traction:

- Seventy-six million YouTube views (the goal was two million)
- 4.5 billion global media impressions (the goal was 250 million)
- 195 percent increase in X (Twitter) followers, and hundreds of thousands of posts
- P&G now holds 50 percent US market share, and 25 percent global market share[31]

2. Dove

PHOTO: Akky Vaishnav on Unsplash

Dove's purpose is to challenge stereotypes, celebrate real beauty, and to help everyone experience beauty and body image positively. Dove's "Choose Beautiful" campaign was crafted to encourage women to choose to feel beautiful. Here again, we see precise alignment with purpose and market-facing messaging. Rather than using their airtime to push inventory, they used it in direct support of their purpose and to send an inspiring message about the beauty in everyone. They focused on telling the world what they believe rather than what they have to sell. And did that cause their sales to fall? Quite the contrary:

- Sales increased from $2.5 billion to $4 billion in the first year of the campaign.

- Dove remains the leading bar and liquid soap brand in the US and the clear market leader in body wash, with around 24 percent share.[32]

3. Nike

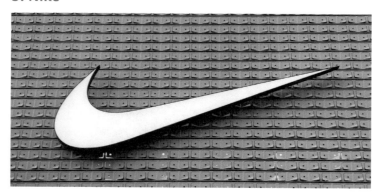

PHOTO: Akky Vaishnav on Unsplash

Nike's purpose statement is "to bring inspiration and innovation to every athlete in the world."

Their "Dream Crazy" campaign encouraged people to reach their highest potential. In choosing Colin Kaepernick, a highly controversial figure at the time, as the spokesperson for the campaign they demonstrated that they were willing to risk alienating buyers to deliver powerful inspiration. As with the Always and Dove examples, Nike's campaign featured no product demos, no key differentiators, and no price guarantees. They chose to focus on purpose. And when they inspired millions of people with that purpose, where did those people go to gear up? They went to Nike:

- 2.7 million brand mentions on social media in the first week of the campaign—a 1,400 percent increase from the prior week

- $43 million worth of earned media exposure

- 30 million views on YouTube for Dream Crazy and 250 million for the full series of Nike Dream ads

- 31 percent increase in online sales for the first week of the campaign

- Nike has a 38.23 percent total market share[33]

When marketing and purpose align it doesn't just attract consumers, it creates fans—people are aligned with you through common beliefs. These cases illustrate that when marketing emanates authentically from a company's purpose, it doesn't just sell products—it resonates with consumers on a deeper level, leading to both commercial success and meaningful engagement.

This is just as true in B2B as it is in B2C (business-to-consumer). Despite all the machinations, governance, and bureaucracy of the corporate landscape, the buying decisions of households and companies alike are still ultimately made by people.

Summing It Up

When a company's marketing efforts are deeply integrated with its purpose, it can lead to exceptional outcomes that exceed traditional business metrics and bolster the company's mission.

Campaigns like Always's "#LikeAGirl" show that focusing on purpose—such as building confidence in young women—can resonate more deeply with audiences than traditional product-focused advertising.

Dove's "Choose Beautiful" campaign highlights the power of purpose in marketing. Promoting positive body image over product features can significantly enhance brand growth and market share.

Nike's "Dream Crazy" campaign demonstrates that taking a bold stand on a company's purpose can engender public respect and lead to a surge in sales and brand visibility, despite potential risks.

Emphasizing purpose rather than products can differentiate a brand in a crowded market, attracting and retaining customers who share similar values. All these examples underline that purpose-driven campaigns can drive not only a company's growth and market dominance but also create a ripple effect of positive social change.

CHAPTER 16

Knowing What A Purpose-Driven Organization Is Not

It's well documented that operating a purpose-driven company can result in a more robust bottom line. Why does this happen? A higher level of innovation, a greater level of workforce performance, and healthier employees are three often-cited reasons. But it's not enough to merely say, "We're a purpose-driven company." You must do the work necessary to make that culture shift with authenticity.

It should be evident by now that what is of more importance is the depth at which purpose has infiltrated every function, action, and conversation. A truly purpose-driven organization makes decisions based on the impact they are seeking to create, not the profits they are hoping to make. They orient their performance incentives around the achievement of their purpose. They put their purpose at the top of their meeting agendas.

Now let's address some areas where companies tend to get hung up.

It's equally important to understand what purpose

is not as it is to know what it is. Author and speaker Zach Mercurio shines a light on six things purpose is not in a blog post[34] of that same name:

- It's not a well-worded statement.
- It's not something you can go and "get" in the future.
- It's not to be "known."
- It's not a fix-all.
- It's not an exercise.
- It's not easy.

This one is the most obvious, but it still bears mentioning that purpose is not just words. Simply crafting a profound purpose statement does not qualify a business as being purpose-driven. Neither does printing it on T-shirts, painting it on the building, or adding it to the company website. Visibility is nice, but action is where the rubber meets the road in the purpose-driven world.

Purpose transcends timelines and strategic objectives. It is the timeless essence that justified your organization's existence when it was founded and will continue to do so into the future.

Ask yourself, what significant void does your company's presence fill in the global tapestry?

Should your so-called purpose waver with the shifting sands of market trends or personal milestones, it is not truly a purpose. Rather, it's a veneer of intention, a strategy for branding or marketing.

Consider this: if crafting a purpose statement or designing a marketing campaign is merely a means to appeal to a particular demographic, like Gen Z, then it's not a genuine purpose. It's a calculated move.

Where Zach says that purpose is not to be "known," he means that a real purpose is a matter of belief, something that "pervades every aspect of our behaviors and attitudes."[35]

That purpose is neither an exercise nor is it easy should both be fairly obvious at this point. Purpose is very much a work-hard-at-it-every-day thing.

Here are two more I would add to Zach's list:

It's not a corporate social responsibility initiative. There's oftentimes confusion on that point. Allocating a portion of proceeds to plant trees to offset carbon emissions from your operations is a great idea; I'm all for it, but it doesn't make your company purpose-driven. Purpose is why your company exists. In fact, many companies have purpose-aligned products and services that could be regarded as being at odds with social and environmental responsibility. But, again, just because a company's purpose isn't a pledge to rescue the planet, doesn't mean it's not valid. If Harley-Davidson wants to make a V12 motorcycle in service to its mission to fulfill dreams of All-American freedom, they may not attract environmentally minded consumers, but it could very well be a bullseye for their purpose.

It's not what you sell. You might sell biodegradable camping sporks for vegans, but that alone doesn't make you a purpose-driven company. It probably just means you talk too much at parties. Your product line is not your purpose, but it should serve as a means to manifest your purpose in the world.

The truth is a company's purpose need not be morally laudable, environmentally responsible, or socially unassailable. It only needs to be genuine.

Let's say you like taking peaceful hikes in your local state park, and you're all about environmental preservation and helping the parks committee keep the trails preserved and that type of thing. Now imagine there's a company out there whose stated purpose is "helping mountain bikers shred more gnar." Has the mountain bike company failed in setting its purpose? Certainly not. They are being 100 percent genuine about what they want to achieve in the world.

We must distinguish between our personal visions for the world and a company's right to define its purpose. Individuals will align with or reject the purpose based on their own values.

I've been involved in many debates about the difference between corporate social responsibility (CSR), environmental sustainability, and purpose. I think it's excellent when an organization's CSR and environmental sustainability work is directly tied to its purpose. That's fantastic. But it's orthogonal to purpose. Purpose is the difference you're seeking to create in the world by being in business, not the thing you're also doing while you're in business.

What if this made-up mountain biking company was making contributions to trail preservation or national parks? Great! But they're different things. I recently read a book on purpose-driven business that recommended companies tie their purpose to pressing, current issues. It asked: "When you look around, what are the pressing issues? What's in the news? What's being debated? Is your company in the game or on the sidelines?"

Personally, I think this guidance is bad because it suggests a company's purpose should be subjected to the whims of public sentiment. Purpose is a North Star, not a meteor. It stays fixed and represents the collective vision of those involved with a company, both internally and externally.

Summing It Up

The heart of a purpose-driven organization is not its marketing slogan or its socially responsible initiatives; it is the genuine, unwavering conviction that guides every action and decision. A true purpose is not swayed by market trends or branding strategies; it is a company's core reason for existing and the unique impact it seeks to make in the world. It's a belief that permeates the culture and inspires every individual within the organization.

As we close this chapter, remember that purpose is the company's compass, remaining constant amid the ever-changing business landscape. It is the authentic embodiment of this purpose that will separate the enduring from the ephemeral in the corporate world. Purpose should be lived, not just stated—deeply woven into the fabric of the company and reflected in the daily work, creating a legacy that stands the test of time.

Now that we have covered the basics of operationalizing purpose, I would like to provide some guidance that will help you along the way in fostering adoption.

CHAPTER 17

Purpose And The Innovation Adoption Curve

Operationalizing purpose is much like any other change or innovation that a company may seek to undertake in that it will require navigating the stages of the innovation adoption curve. Along the journey to purpose, you'll run into the different personalities of the curve: the innovators, the early adopters, the middle majority, the late majority, and the traditionalists—sometimes called the laggards or skeptics.

Whether it's a company, a target market, or an entire nation, any group of more than a handful of people is going to have folks representing every tier of the adoption curve.

Why is it important to be aware of this? Because to succeed with innovation, it is very helpful to be aware of the populations you're going to run into and the roles they serve. As you introduce a purpose operationalization plan into an organization, you'll certainly find people who are eager to jump on board for the pure excitement of innovation, but no matter how inspiring your purpose or how well-crafted you plan, you'll also find people in your organization who'll have their foot on the brake.

What I want leaders to be aware of is that when they encounter people who use language like, "We can't afford to spend money on that. We don't have time for it. We tried that before. We've got more important things to do," etc., those sentiments derive from a protective energy and can, in fact, serve a very important purpose.

Before I knew better, I used to view institutionalists mostly as friction in the system. I used to think, "If they would only just get out of the way, we could make some real progress." But now I know that institutionalists play a vital role in the life cycle of innovation and in the ultimate success of the companies they work for. Without cautious skepticism and the careful preservation of legacy systems, companies would fall into chaos.

Now there is such a thing as too much protection, too much skepticism. This is where you can picture Ralphie's little brother from *A Christmas Story*, who's bundled up by his mother with so much clothing and padding he can't move. You become immobile with too much caution.

Just to provide a visual that will keep me clear of copyright entanglements, here's Chat GPT's attempt to recreate Ralphie in his immobilizing winter garb. Honestly, it's even better in the movie. Definitely worth a watch.

But you can also have such a thing as too little caution. Consider the character Borat in his "mankini," which I think collectively everyone can agree was probably not a good move, but I'm sure he enjoyed (mostly) great freedom of movement even while he would have been blocked at the door from many places of business.

I did have a hope to include an image of Borat from the famous and hilarious "mankini" scene, but that would also require studio permission. I was also quite hesitant to attempt it with a generative AI as I didn't want to see anything I couldn't unsee - risky territory for sure. Alas, I did push past my reservations only to be told "I'm unable to create an image that would mimic the extremely revealing nature of that outfit," which honestly is a more hilarious outcome in my opinion. Moving on.

Let's take a closer look at the five personalities in the context of adopting a purpose-driven business model within a company.

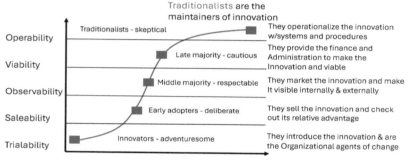

Innovators

The first approximately 2.5 percent of a group to adopt a new idea, innovators are venturesome, risk-takers, and interested in new ideas. Pioneers of purpose-driven business embrace the risk inherent in blazing a trail. They are the vanguards, eager to infuse every aspect of their operation with their core mission. Their ambition is not merely to sell, but to catalyze transformative change by aligning their business practices with their values. This commitment to purpose is an innovation in and of itself, transcending conventional business metrics.

For such leaders, integrating purpose is not a strategy; it's a fundamental shift in corporate identity. This steadfast dedication to a cause can often position them at the fringes of traditional business circles, with their forward-thinking approaches perceived as unconventional or even disruptive by the established order.

Yet, their role is crucial. In the ecosystem of an organization, these innovators may be scarce, but their influence is profound. When they successfully embed their purpose into their business model, they not only pioneer a new paradigm but also set a benchmark for authenticity and impact. Their validation serves as a beacon, guiding and assuring others in the marketplace of the viability and critical importance of a purpose beyond profit.

Early Adopters

The next 13.5 percent or so to adopt an innovation, early adopters are opinion leaders who are concerned about being ahead of the curve.

Early adopters are the visionaries who recognize the transformative potential of aligning profit with purpose. Once the pioneers have laid the groundwork, these insightful leaders are quick to embrace this ethos, seeing it not as a trend but as a competitive differentiator that resonates with a growing consumer desire for meaningful engagement with brands.

THE RACE TO RELEVANCE

Early adopters integrate purpose into their businesses to set themselves apart, keenly aware that doing so can redefine their industry and elevate their standing. They are willing to invest time and resources, seeing the long-term value beyond immediate gains. Their adoption serves as a critical phase in refining the purpose-driven model, smoothing out the initial challenges, and adapting it for broader application.

As catalysts for change, these early adopters don't just adopt new business innovations—they become the case studies and success stories that validate the movement. Their endorsement and adjustments pave the way for the purpose-driven approach to reach the mainstream, proving that a business can thrive by putting its raison d'être at the forefront of its strategy.

Early Majority

The next 34 percent adopt an innovation; the early majority of members adopt new ideas before the average person but are rarely trail-blazers.

The early majority are the pragmatic artists who adopt this model when they see it can solve real-world issues and align with their core operations. They wait for the initial idea of purpose integration to be vetted and proven by the innovators and early adopters before they commit.

This group isn't looking for radical change; rather,

they want a turnkey approach to purpose that fits seamlessly into their existing structures. They prioritize solutions that have been demonstrated to work, are endorsed by peers, and align with industry benchmarks. This mainstream segment wants to know that embedding purpose into their business will enhance what they're already doing without causing significant disruption or requiring substantial new learning.

For the early majority, the implementation of purpose must be simple, with clear benefits such as improved brand reputation, customer loyalty, or employee satisfaction that can lead to tangible returns. They're swayed by evidence that a purpose-driven strategy can be cost-effective or offer a quick return on investment.

Given their numbers, persuading the early majority is crucial; they represent the tipping point for a purpose-driven approach to become the standard. Their buy-in is what allows for the transition from a niche trend to an established business practice, ensuring sustained growth and profitability in the market.

Late Majority

The 34 percent of the group to the right of the mean, late majority members are skeptical of change and will only adopt an innovation after it has been tried by the middle majority.

The late majority steps in once the purpose-driven paradigm in a company is well-established and almost universally accepted. They approach purpose integration cautiously, often motivated by the growing consensus and the fear of being perceived as outdated. They favor stability over innovation and will commit to purpose-driven practices when there's ample proof that these strategies are the new norm.

This group seeks reassurance through high levels of support, training, and evidence of best practices. They may also look for certifications or standards that validate the company's commitment to purpose as a safeguard against potential risks associated with change.

Representing a significant portion of the market, the late majority's adoption is less about seizing opportunities and more about conforming to industry transformations. When they do engage with purpose-driven models, it's typically because the practices have been refined, the risks minimized, and the pathway for implementation is clear and well-trodden.

When catering to the late majority, the key is to offer straightforward, low-risk entry points into purpose-driven practices. The late majority's engagement is a sign of a purpose-driven business model reaching full maturity and acceptance.

Laggards/Institutionalists

The last 16 percent want to adopt an innovation; laggards are bound by tradition and very conservative.

Laggards—referred to here as "institutionalists"—are the final group to engage and the true mark of an innovation reaching operationalization. They cling to traditional business models and are the most resistant to adopting the ethos of purpose over profit. They typically only transition to purpose-driven methods when market shifts, consumer demands, or corporate edict leave them no choice, or when their conventional strategies become untenably outdated and ineffective.

Institutionalists approach change with a high degree of skepticism. They prioritize legacy systems and views, often questioning the authenticity or financial logic behind purpose-driven approaches. Their move toward purpose is often reactive rather than proactive, driven by a need to catch up rather than a desire to lead or innovate.

To engage with this group, it's necessary to present purpose-driven business as not just an emotional choice but as a pragmatic one linked to survival in the modern market. Change management strategies must be employed to ease their transition, using language that resonates with their preference for tradition and risk avoidance. Regrettably, preaching the virtues of a laudable purpose may simply not cut it for this group. Demonstrating that a purpose-driven approach can revitalize traditional business practices may be crucial to winning their trust and participation.

Institutionalists can be a tricky group to get on board, and it can be easy for champions of change to focus perhaps too much energy on achieving buy-in from this group before taking action toward goals. Waiting for an endorsement from this group can prevent an otherwise well-crafted initiative from gaining the necessary momentum as it progresses through the more adventurous and willing groups. In many cases a lack of active resistance may be the best green light you get from institutionalists in the early stages.

In the long run their eventual adoption is a significant marker, signaling that purpose-driven business has become so embedded in the commercial landscape that it's no longer optional but a fundamental aspect of staying relevant.

Summing It Up

Adopting a purpose-driven approach in business mirrors the innovation adoption curve, encountering varying mindsets from innovators to laggards. The key is to be aware of how they think, what motivates them, and what behaviors you can expect from them along the way. Innovators boldly infuse purpose into their operations, setting a transformative precedent. Early adopters then take the baton, demonstrating the competitive edge that purpose brings. The early majority follows, integrating purpose pragmatically within existing structures, while the late majority waits for purpose-driven practices to become the standard before committing. Lastly, the laggards, or institutionalists, reluctantly adapt out of necessity. Each group's response—from eager embrace to cautious skepticism—plays a critical role in the widespread adoption and success of purpose within a company, balancing innovation with the preservation of core systems.

Now that we have this frame of reference for purpose, what is the next logical step? That would be living with purpose, which is explored in part III of this book.

PART III

LIVING
WITH PURPOSE

CHAPTER 18

Preparing For Growth

If I have done my job well in the prior chapters, at this point, you will be feeling inspired to transition your company to being purpose-driven and confident that you have a path to do so. Should you decide to move forward, there is some additional guidance I would like to offer.

As illustrated in part I, companies that effectively transition to a purpose-driven business model generally see stronger growth than conventional model companies. One key bit of advice that I offer to all leaders who are about to experience accelerated growth is to "replace yourself as quickly as you can."

Prior to my first experience in a rapidly growing company, I had believed that the key to being a valuable member of the team was to be the only person on the team that could do what I could do. That belief was effectively shattered when I got my first taste of working in a fast-growth environment. It quickly became evident to me that we were going to need multiple people capable of everything I knew how to do and so much more.

The way to be valuable in a high-growth company is to be capable of making people valuable.

Share what you know. Give them your best tools, templates, and processes. Document your decision trees. Trust your team to make decisions. Give them authority. Create a positive environment that includes the support and resources people need to be successful and grow. Work with your team to develop strategies for building resilience and adaptability.

It is much easier to deal with growth proactively than to respond to it reactively. If you wait until you have no time left to duplicate your abilities and capacities in others, you'll be too late.

The data is clear: a shift to purpose is a shift to growth. Plan accordingly.

CHAPTER 19

Beware The Dilution Of Purpose

When confined to the hands of a select few, purpose risks becoming a mere slogan rather than a company's living, breathing ethos. For purpose to be truly effective, it must be deeply ingrained in the organization's culture and operations, resonating with individuals at every level.

Purpose is like gravity in that the further from the source you are the weaker the force will be. If purpose is perceived as a top-down mandate, it may fail to inspire the genuine buy-in necessary for transformational change. Instead, purpose should be democratized—felt and understood as a personal mission by everyone from the boardroom to the front lines. If everyone owns purpose, the gravity of it will be felt all around.

I have had some difficulty in verifying if it's true, but the John F. Kennedy at NASA story has become legend and is a beautiful encapsulation of what a purpose-driven organization looks like. It goes something like the following.

Allegedly, in 1962, JFK made his first visit to the NASA Space Center for a tour and was being guided

throughout the facility. He passed a janitor in a hallway and stopped to ask him, "What do you do here?" And the janitor said, "I'm helping to put a man on the moon."

When everyone in every role, no matter how seemingly removed from the end result, understands how their function serves the organization's purpose, that's a very powerful indicator that they have made major strides toward operationalizing their purpose.

Suggestions for broadening ownership and keeping the connection to purpose alive include the following:

- *Inclusive purpose development.* Involve employees in determining the actions that are needed to operationalize purpose within the company. Have department leaders take their teams through the same "exit ticket" process the leadership team experienced when they made their action commitments. Ownership starts when individuals feel their input matters.

- *Purpose champions.* Establish a network of purpose champions across various departments and teams, encompassing individuals who are passionate about the company's mission and can inspire their colleagues.

- *Storytelling.* Encourage the sharing of personal stories that reflect how individuals and teams live out the company's purpose in their daily work. This storytelling can take place in meetings, on internal platforms, or at company events.

- *Purpose-driven recognition.* Implement a recognition program that rewards actions and decisions that exemplify the company's purpose. This will recognize and reinforce purposeful behavior at all levels.

- *Bringing employees on board purposefully.* Ensure that the process for bringing new employees on board is infused with the company's purpose, setting the expectation that everyone is a custodian of the company's mission.

- *Purpose in performance.* Integrate the company's purpose into performance reviews and goal setting. Employees should understand how their roles and objectives align with the broader mission.

- *Purpose education.* Offer training and development opportunities that help employees understand the company's purpose and how they can contribute to it.

- *Purpose in decision-making.* Equip employees with decision-making frameworks that prioritize the company's purpose, ensuring that even small decisions are made with the mission in mind.

By weaving purpose into the fabric of the company in these ways, it becomes a collective endeavor that is lived out in the actions and decisions of each individual, thereby fortifying it against the dilution that can come with hierarchical ownership.

Summing It Up

Embracing a purpose-driven model means transcending traditional corporate hierarchies to allow purpose to permeate every level of an organization. Purpose should be a force felt by all, from the boardroom to the operational floors. When even the janitor believes their work contributes to a monumental goal—as illustrated by the legendary story of JFK's interaction at NASA—the company's purpose is truly operationalized.

To embed purpose deeply, involve all employees in its development and celebrate its embodiment in everyday actions. Foster a culture where purpose-driven behavior is recognized, new hires are inducted with the company's mission in mind, and performance reviews reflect alignment with purpose. Through training and clear decision-making frameworks, empower each individual to be a custodian of purpose.

When each member of the company, regardless of their role, is a vibrant advocate for the mission, the purpose becomes more than a statement—it becomes the very essence of the company's identity and success.

CHAPTER 20

Embracing Purpose—
The Global Future Of Business

In this journey through the necessity of purpose in modern business, we've touched on everything from the operational implications to the transformative power of purpose-driven leadership. The evidence and stories shared across these pages not only illustrate the importance of purpose, but also demonstrate its profound impact on organizations, employees, and society at large.

As we draw this exploration to a close, it's crucial to underscore that embracing purpose is not merely a strategy, but a fundamental shift in how businesses must operate in the modern world. The era of businesses operating solely for profit is waning. Today, the most successful and resilient organizations are those driven by a clear, compelling purpose that resonates with their employees, customers, and the broader community.

Purpose goes beyond slogans and mission statements—it must be woven into the very fabric of a company's culture. It is about aligning every business decision and innovation with a deeper mission, ensuring that every employee understands and is motivated by the why behind their daily tasks. This alignment is not just beneficial; it is essential for sustainable success in an increasingly complex and volatile business landscape.

Through many examples, we've seen that purpose can drive incredible growth and transformation. Purpose mobilizes people, fosters innovation, and builds resilience. It attracts talent and inspires loyalty in ways that traditional incentives cannot match. In a world where the public is increasingly scrutinizing corporate practices, a genuine commitment to purpose can enhance trust and brand reputation.

To leaders and change makers who are steering their ships through the choppy waters of industry, remember that purpose is your North Star. It provides direction guiding you through challenges and toward meaningful achievements. The race to relevance is not just about speed; it is about depth—the depth of your commitment to a purpose that transcends economic gains and contributes positively to the world.

As you continue to navigate the future, let purpose be your compass. Let it guide your strategies, inform your decisions, and inspire your people. The path to a truly purpose-driven business is neither quick nor easy, but it is undoubtedly rewarding. By embedding purpose into your core, you not only enhance your competitive edge but also contribute to a more equitable, sustainable, and prosperous world.

Thank you for joining me on this exploration of purpose in business. May the insights garnered here fuel your journey toward a more purposeful and impactful future. Here's to not just surviving but thriving in the race to relevance—may your purpose illuminate the way forward.

Now it's your turn.

Do great things.

APPENDIX

Acknowledgments

My deepest gratitude to those who helped me along the way:

Sarah Armstrong for keeping me true to my own purpose.

Rob Walters for helping me to believe I could write a book.

Henry Devries for adapting the ramblings of a lunatic into coherent ideas.

Erin Comfort for lending her pedagogical brilliance.

Julia Fox for daily encouragement and support.

About The Author

Colt is a twenty-year, Finny award-winning marketing and communications (MarCom) exec who has been featured in *Forbes*, Entrepreneur, EXHIBITOR magazine, and Fast Company. Founder of the B2B growth consultancy Scrappy AF, Colt now supports multiple nine-figure B2B brands across multiple industries. He is a guest presenter for MBA programs in California universities and a sought-after speaker at conferences, workshops, and events around the world.

Colt's Thought Followship strategy, featured in *Forbes*, has raised the benchmark for prospect engagement and high-value content generation in B2B marketing.

Through his consultancy, he helps young organizations capture market share from industry incumbents and supports established businesses in accelerating growth and building pathways into new markets. Colt has spent his entire career where the rubber meets the road between solution development on one side and marketing and sales on the other side. This experience has enabled him to combine strong strategies with creative execution to help businesses and sectors grow fast while spending less.

Colt lives in Santa Rosa, California, with his son and partner and counts himself among those who shred the gnar on both mountain bike and snowboard.

Purpose Workshops

PURPOSE-DRIVEN
business workshop

with Colt Briner

The pains of business without purpose

- Struggling to attract, retain and engage top talent in your sector.
- Rapid disruption is causing your organization to continuously pivot.
- Your brand presence lacks the magnetic energy to attract new business.
- Your innovation efforts are slow, expensive and hit & miss.
- Your customer loyalty is on the decline.

Results you can expect from going purpose-driven

- Attract, retain and deeply engage top talent
- Higher customer loyalty
- Stronger innovation from every department
- Increased sales and shareholder value

How to craft, communicate and operationalize purpose for sustainable success.

In this engaging, transformative and fun workshop, Colt will personally guide your leadership team in aligning on your visionary purpose and building out your purpose operationalization plan - the path to transitioning your company to a purpose-driven model of business.

You will learn

The incredible results being achieved by businesses that effectively operationalize their purpose and the secrets of their success

How to co-create a truly visionary purpose that aligns with the personal purpose of each of your staff members

The psychological drivers that make purpose such a powerful force in business

How to foster the critical mindset shifts that power purpose-driven individuals, teams and organizations

The 6 steps for effectively operationalizing purpose in a company

The 3 pitfalls of purpose driven business and how to avoid them

How to use purpose to engage and build strong relationships with your top prospects

How to strengthen your organizations capacity for innovation

About Colt: Author, speaker and 20-year MarCom executive. Colt's mission is to accelerate the world's transition to the next era of business: one that is driven by purpose. As CCO for a Cincinnati BPO, he helped to take them from a $60M valuation to $2B, outrank all competitors on Indeed and Glassdoor, and capture 60% market share in just 30 months using a purpose-driven business framework. Now he teaches leadership teams how to transform their companies into purpose-driven powerhouses.

Let's talk about where your company is at and the transition you are looking to create. Then we can plan a workshop that's custom tailored for your specific needs.

Schedule a call with Colt:

What people are saying:

Don Schwartz
MBA Professor
Sonoma State University

"Colt speaks with a compelling message and an engaging style. He makes it simple to understand that which others make complicated."

Brent Rollins
CEO
RSi

"Colt's ability to execute and deliver results is unmatched."

Erin Avery
CEO
ConcernCenter

"Colt has innovative and personable ways of connecting and does so in a seamless and genuine way. Five star + recommendation!"

April Langford
CEO
RevCycleMatch

"Colt always achieves outstanding results and provides thoughtful guidance."

Brent Lockhart
President
Ratermann Manufacturing

"Our entire team walked away with a new found energy and a 100% commitment to our being a purpose driven organization."

Laurence Haughton
NYT bestselling Author
"The Reinventors"

"Colt's workshop is packed with wisdom addressing the known pitfalls: giving your team clarity, tons of buy-in and maintaining everyone's momentum."

Works Cited
And Author's Comments

1   Eric C. Schneider et al., *Mirror, Mirror 2021: Reflecting Poorly: Health Care in the U.S. Compared to Other High-Income Countries* (New York: Commonwealth Fund, August 21, 2021), https://www.commonwealthfund.org/sites/default/files/2021-08/Schneider_Mirror_Mirror_2021.pdf.

2   Putting Purpose to Work: A Study of Purpose in the Workplace (PwC, June 2016), https://www.pwc.com/us/en/about-us/corporate-responsibility/assets/pwc-putting-purpose-to-work-purpose-survey-report.pdf.

3   Jim Hemerling et al., "For Corporate Purpose to Matter You've Got to Measure It," BCG, August 16, 2018, https://www.bcg.com/publications/2018/corporate-purpose-to-matter-measure-it.

4   "Consumers care about sustainability—and back it up with their wallets," NIQ, nielseniq.com, February 6, 2023, https://nielseniq.com/global/en/insights/report/2023/consumers-care-about-sustainability-and- back-it-up-with-their-wallets/

5   "The Business Case for Purpose", *Harvard Business Review*, 2019, https://hbr.org/resources/pdfs/comm/ey/19392HBRReportEY.pdf

6   "Sir Christopher Wren and the Three Bricklayers," Brownleeglobal.com, April 7, 2021, https://www.

brownleeglobal.com/sir-christopher-wren-and-the-
story-of-three-bricklayers/

7   "Another Deloitte Survey Says "Purpose" is Just
as Important as Pay (Yeah Right)," GoingConcern.
com, October 27, 2022, https://www.goingconcern.
com/deloitte-survey-talent-considers-purpose-
important/#:~:text=A%20Deloitte%20survey%20
of%20over,their%20salary%20and%20benefits%20
package

8   "Research: 3 Employee Experiences Most Likely to
Drive Retention," Great Place to Work, January 30,
2024, https://www.greatplacetowork.com/press-
releases/employee-experiences-drive-retention

9   Carlos Rivis, "The Predicted Fate of Fortune 500
Companies: A Visionary Perspective," Linked-In.com,
July 22, 2023, https://www.linkedin.com/pulse/
predicted-fate-fortune-500-companies-visionary-
carlo-rivis/

10   Alex Hill, Liz Mellon, and Jules Goddard, "How Winning
Organizations Last 100 years," Harvard Business Review,
September 27, 2018, https://hbr.org/2018/09/how-
winning-organizations-last-100-years

11   Gallup State of the Workforce Report 2023, " From
Suffering to Thriving," Gallup.com, 2024, https://
www.gallup.com/workplace/349484/state-of-the-
global-workplace.aspx

12   Raj Sisodia and Jag Sheth, Firms of Endearment,(Upper
Saddle River, NJ: Pearson FT Press, 2014)

13 Nick Craig and Scott A. Snook, "From Purpose to Impact," *Harvard Business Review*, May 2014, https://hbr.org/2014/05/from-purpose-to-impact

14 Jim Collins and Jerry I Porras, *Built to Last: Successful Habits of Visionary Companies,* (New York: Harper Business, 2011)

15 Aaron Mack, "Purpose-Driven Companies do More Good—and More Business," Firespring.com, March 14, 2023, https://firespring.com/powered-by-purpose/purpose-driven-companies-do-more-good-and-more-business/#:~:text=Deloitte percent20found percent20purpose percent2Ddriven percent20brands,higher percent20levels percent20of percent20workforce percent20retention

16 Adeline de Oliveira, "Purpose-Driven Business: How Purpose Drives Success," *Performance Insight Blog*, Proaction International, May 8, 2023, https://blog.proactioninternational.com/en/purpose-driven-business-how-purpose-drives-success.

17 Lydia Saad, "Eight in 10 Americans Afflicted by Stress," Gallup.com, December 20, 2017, https://news.gallup.com/poll/224336/eight-americans-afflicted-stress.aspx

18 John Masefield, "Sea-Fever," in *Salt-Water Poems and Ballads* (New York: Macmillan, 1913), p. 65.

19 Judy Cameron, Katherine M. Banko, and W. David Pierce, "Pervasive Negative Effects of Rewards on Intrinsic Motivation: The Myth Continues," *The Behavior Analyst* 24, no. 1 (Spring 2001): 1–44, doi: 10.1007/BF03392017.

20   Alfie Kohn, "Why Incentive Plans Cannot Work," *Harvard Business Review,* September-October 2009, https://hbr.org/1993/09/why-incentive-plans-cannot-work

21   Shanna Carpenter, "Dan Pink at TEDGlobal 2009, Running Notes from Session 12," TEDBlog.com, July 24, 2009, https://blog.ted.com/dan_pink_at_ted/

22   Edward L. Deci, "Effects of Externally Mediated Rewards on Intrinsic Motivation, *Journal of Personality and Social Psychology* 18, no. 1, April 1971: 105–115. https://doi.org/10.1037/h0030644.

23   Dan Pink, "The Puzzle of Motivation," TedGlobal.com, July 2009, https://www.ted.com/talks/dan_pink_the_puzzle_of_motivation?subtitle=en

24   Karl Duncker, "On Problem-Solving," trans. L. S. Lees, *Psychological Monographs* 58, no. 5 (1945): i–113, https://doi.org/10.1037/h0093599

25   John Kounios and Mark Beeman, "How Incentives Hinder Innovation," *The Psych Report*, September 3, 2015, https://behavioralscientist.org/how-incentives-hinder- innovation-creativity/

26   "Pink's Autonomy, Mastery and Purpose Framework," MindTools, accessed July 24, 2024, https://www.mindtools.com/asmdp60/pinks-autonomy-mastery-and-purpose-framework.

27   Simon Sinek, *The Infinite Game* (New York: Portfolio/ Penguin, 2019).

28   Seth Godin, *This Is Marketing: You Can't Be Seen Until You Learn to See* (New York: Portfolio/Penguin, 2018).

29 Marshall B Rosenberg, PhD and Deepak Chopra, *Non-Violent Communication: A Language of Life: Life-Changing Tools for Healthy Relationships*, (Encinitas, CA: PuddleDancer Press, 2015)

30 Simon Sinek, *Start with Why: How Great Leaders Inspire Everyone to Take Action* (Toronto: Portfolio, 2009), p.18.

31 "Case Study: Always #LikeAGirl," Campaign.com, October 12, 2015, https://www.campaignlive.co.uk/article/case-study-always-likeagirl/1366870

32 SharadhaR, "An Analysis of Dove's Breakthrough Marketing Campaign, 'Real Beauty'," Medium.com, September 2, 2020, https://medium.com/hustle-monk/doves-breakthrough-marketing-campaign-involved-empowerment-of-real-women-ad2734c0188a

33 Jay Leonard, "5 Numbers From Nike's Recent 'Dream Crazy' Campaign That Confirm It's Smashing Success," Business-2-Community.com. September 10, 2018, https://www.business2community.com/public-relations/5-numbers-from-nikes-recent-dream-crazy-campaign-that-confirm-its-smashing-success-02117687

34 Zach Mercurio, "Here Are 6 Things 'Purpose' Is Not," *Zach's Blog*, September 21, 2016, https://www.zachmercurio.com/2016/09/here-are-6-things-purpose-is-not/.

35 Mecurio, "Here Are 6 Things," https://www.zachmercurio.com/2016/09/here-are-6-things-purpose-is-not/.

Made in the USA
Columbia, SC
15 March 2025